RAILS THROUGH THE WEST

Front Cover

Upper: Quintessential Western Rail Corridor: B145 has the very last Sligo–Limerick
goods train on 30 October 1975. This train had left Sligo Quay at 1020 but did not arrive
in Claremorris until 1735, as a result of severe delays in loading goods from a factory at
Swinford. Only one more public train will operate over the line past this point (between
Collooney and Leyney*) – this will be the northbound equivalent of this train several
hours later.

** 'Leyney' was the name given to this station by the railway companies but it is more commonly known
as Coolaney.*

Lower: Preserved J15 class 0-6-0 No 186 heads past Labane castle on 11 June 1977, with a
Railway Preservation Society of Ireland railtour near Ardrahan. This was the annual RPSI
long weekend tour – now an institution in the Irish railway calendar. With the re-opening
of the Limerick–Athenry section to passenger traffic, they will again admire this castle and
the local scenery which is so typical of the whole route.

Published 2012 by
Colourpoint Books
Colourpoint House, Jubilee Business Park
Jubilee Road, Newtownards, BT23 4YH
Tel: 028 9182 6339
Fax: 028 9182 1900
E-mail: info@colourpoint.co.uk
Web: www.colourpoint.co.uk

First Edition
First Impression

Designed by April Sky Design, Newtownards
Tel: 028 9182 7195
Web: www.aprilsky.co.uk

Printed by W&G Baird Ltd, Antrim

ISBN 978-1-78073-006-6

Rear cover: B133 in original livery enters Tuam with a short goods train en route from
Claremorris to Limerick about 1962. The grey and yellow livery was unique to these locomotives,
and once due for their first repaint they acquired the standard 'black and tan' livery.
At least one example still wore the livery shown as late as 1968 or 1969. *(John Edgington)*

About the authors: Jonathan Beaumont and Barry Carse are both lifelong railway enthusiasts who have
an extensive knowledge of the 'rails through the west' of Ireland. Jonathan Beaumont has previously
published *Rails to Achill* and *Achillbeg: The Life of an Island* (both Oakwood Press) as well as many articles.
Barry Carse is a well known and accomplished railway photographer with an extensive collection of images from across Ireland.

RAILS THROUGH THE WEST

LIMERICK TO SLIGO

An illustrated journey on the Western Rail Corridor

JONATHAN BEAUMONT AND BARRY CARSE

Dedicated to the railwaymen and women who worked the Limerick–Sligo line

Claremorris, June 1974: A driver and signalman pose for the camera prior to
departure of the afternoon train to Ballina.

CONTENTS

Route Map 6

Introduction 7

Limerick–Athenry 9

Athenry–Galway 44

Athenry–Claremorris 49

Claremorris–Sligo 70

Claremorris–Ballina 96

Tuam Sugar Beet Factory 106

Knock Specials 114

CIÉ Working Time Table June to September 1961 120

Track Plans 122

Locomotives Used on this Route 127

'Western Rail Corridor' Re-Opening 129

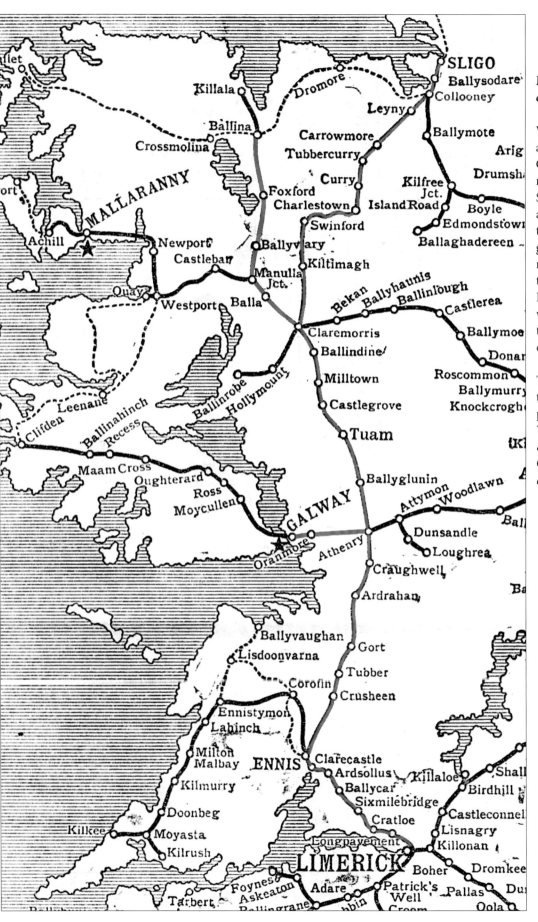

Map showing routes covered in the book

What is now known as the 'Western Rail Corridor' is the main route from Limerick to Sligo. On the basis that after 1963, all passenger trains were diverted to go to Ballina, and in recent times the new train service is from Limerick to Galway, we have included these sections for completeness.

The map is from the 1901 timetable published by the Waterford, Limerick & Western Railway Company. (*Author's collection*)

INTRODUCTION

The long cross-country railway route from Sligo to Limerick is nowadays known as the 'Western Rail Corridor' (WRC), a name which is of recent origin and has come about as a result of post-closure efforts to 'brand' it as a single entity, to assist in heightening public awareness of campaigns to reopen it fully. However, it was not always thus.

The line was built over a period by several different railway companies, with Ennis being reached from Limerick in 1859. Athenry was reached by 1869, and the section beyond there to Claremorris received its first through train in 1894. Several small railway companies had been formed to carry out these piecemeal extensions, but, after 1 November 1872, the Waterford & Limerick Railway Company (W&L) worked the train services for them. In October 1895 the line reached Carrignagat Junction, near Collooney, Co Sligo. At this point, the line joined the Midland Great Western railway's line from Dublin to Sligo, so the W&L company obtained powers to run its trains from there over the last six miles into Sligo. The WRC was born, and by degrees the small companies involved in building it were absorbed into the W&L. In 1896, in order to recognise the fact that the Waterford & Limerick Railway had this long straggling route into the west under their control, the company was renamed the Waterford, Limerick & Western Railway.

Only five years later, the larger and more southerly neighbour, the Great Southern & Western Railway, took over the WLWR, and the WRC became a remote western outpost of the Dublin-controlled GSWR for the future years.

In 1925, the GSWR was itself incorporated into the Great Southern Railways, an amalgamation of all railway companies whose lines lay entirely within the recently created Irish Free State. Twenty years elapsed before the creation of Córas Iompair Éireann (CIÉ), which was an amalgamation of the GSR with the canal companies and the Dublin tram and bus systems. CIÉ was nationalised in 1950, thus bringing the WRC under state control.

As a small part of what came to be almost an all-Ireland public transport system, the WRC was neglected over the years, though to be fair to the GSR and CIÉ, the country was poor. Little money was available to invest in main lines, let alone secondary ones.

By the mid-1950s, the line was operating (like many rural routes in Ireland) with steam locomotives and passenger carriages dating from the 1880s onwards. The late arrival of diesel railcars in the 1950s did little to revive the line's fortunes, as there was by this stage only one passenger train per day in each direction over the whole route. However, goods trains remained busy.

The early 1960s brought major changes. Passenger trains were discontinued over the 'Burma Road' section from Claremorris to Collooney, and the daily passenger train started operating between Limerick and Ballina instead of Limerick and Sligo. Steam locomotives disappeared from the line also, though since the first diesels arrived in the mid-1950s they had become scarcer. 1963 was, in fact, the year in which CIÉ became the first state-owned railway system in Europe to dispense with steam locomotives altogether. The first of the many American built diesel locomotives appeared – these were the B121 class in their distinctive (but short lived) grey and yellow livery.

Passenger traffic continued to decline over the next ten years; by the time the author travelled on the line in the early 1970s the passenger train had but a single coach and guard's van, hauled by a main line diesel locomotive.

As before, goods traffic remained buoyant, with some small intermediate stations handling a considerable amount of freight of all types. However, the line became alive in the autumn, when the annual sugar beet 'campaign' started, and huge loads of beet were taken by rail from many distant points over the line into Tuam Sugar Factory. This required special trains, and shunting locomotives were allocated to Tuam for the duration of the beet campaign, generally November to late January.

From 3 November 1975, even the remaining goods

train was discontinued between Claremorris and Carrignagat Junction, leaving the 'Burma Road' derelict and closed. It remains thus to this day, though the heavily overgrown track bed was cleared in 2007 to maintain the right of way and repair fences.

In 1976, the Limerick to Ballina through passenger train was discontinued, leaving only a daily passenger train between Limerick and Ennis. However, this was to succumb a year or so later, leaving the entire route without a single passenger train.

In 1988, a limited passenger service was re-introduced between Limerick and Ennis – perhaps the start of the route's revival. This proved a success and brand new diesel railcars were eventually transferred onto this service. The Ennis–Athenry line had become impassable with weeds and general dereliction, while the Athenry to Claremorris route had actually been physically disconnected at Athenry after the main line track there (part of the Galway–Dublin route) had been relaid in 2003.

Elsewhere the picture was less encouraging as CIÉ began to withdraw from carriage of general goods. By the late 1980s, except for beet in season, little travelled north of Ennis apart from through traffic between Claremorris or Ballina and Limerick. The intermediate stations were boarded up, left to become covered in weeds, and in some cases demolished – if not by the railway company, vandals and time did the job just as well. Some became private houses, and Kiltimagh station became the town's museum. Two old carriages destined for this museum became the last train north of Claremorris.

Work started in 2007 on relaying the track between Ennis and Athenry with a view to extending the new passenger service to enable it to operate between Limerick and Galway via Athenry. This new service commenced in 2010.

The rest of the WRC remains derelict and unusable, though plans exist to extend the passenger services to Tuam in future years. Given the extensive worldwide financial woes of the post 2008 period, one can only wonder when this might take place.

Almost since the last passenger trains ran, a local campaign started to re-open the entire route to passenger traffic. This manifested itself in the emergence of a local pressure group called 'West=On=Track', whose aim is to achieve this.

At the start of the second decade of the twenty-first Century, a century after the GSWR took over the line's operation, the Western Rail Corridor is a display of its own history. At the south end, a busy and well used passenger service operates with modern trains over well maintained track; in the middle, renewal work is under way or planned, and at the northern end all is quiet, save for the birds in the trees which grow between the rails.

It is hoped that future years will bring the whole route, or much of it, back to life again.

What follows is a portrait of the line in its Indian Summer, with the colour photography of Barry Carse allowing the line to come to life on these pages. The photographs span the period from the late 1960s to 2011.

We hope that this collection will revive memories for the line's users, for local people, and others with an interest in this unique and picturesque railway.

LIMERICK–ATHENRY

It is appropriate that we begin our journey in Limerick, the largest population centre along this route. Limerick was the Headquarters of the Waterford, Limerick & Western Railway, who operated the line prior to amalgamation into the Great Southern Railway.

Above: In 1961, three major railway societies combined to organise what was probably the most ambitious railway enthusiast tour of Ireland ever undertaken. The Irish Railway Record Society was joined in this venture by the Stephenson Locomotive Society and the Railway Correspondence and Travel Society from the UK, and here we see this tour in Limerick station, the starting point of our odyssey northwards to Sligo in this book. The locomotive is J15 class 0-6-0 No 125. The late Billy Lohan, a former driver on the line, recalled that when he started work in the late 1910s at Tuam, the shed there had an allocation of six of these locomotives, which were used on all types of traffic.

The track to Foynes, not yet closed but by now little used, curves away to the left behind the photographer. A slight film of rust on the surface of the rails in the foreground illustrates this. The signal cabin is of interest in showing a standard Great Southern Railways bilingual sign – these were still commonplace then. The coaching stock in the station includes the standard 'tin vans' used on many passenger trains at the time. Their unpainted finish became very drab and dirty looking, as can be seen. At least the carriages (of late 1950s origin – quite new at this time) are in the standard CIÉ green livery of the day. The green paint extended beyond carriages – station woodwork, as on the signal box, also received this colour. Semaphore signals are the order of the day: no colour lights here. *(John Langford)*

Above: In the mid-1970s, two 141-class locomotives lead a special train from Limerick to Claremorris (for Knock Shrine), past Limerick Check Signal Cabin. The leading loco, B144, is in the original 'black and tan' livery, while the second one has recently been repainted in the 'orange and black' (without white lines) used between 1972 and 1987. The signalling is of interest: we see a colour light signal to the left of the train, along with a ground semaphore, while behind the first locomotive semaphore bracket signals may be seen. The paintwork on the cabin has seen better days, as has the painted GSR sign above its end windows. By the 1970s, the universal green paint on railway buildings had largely been replaced by grey.

Opposite: Loco 123 leads loco 131 on the 1700 'logs' – a train of timber from Ennis to Waterford, which has just come in from Ennis and is about to pass Limerick Check cabin. The Foynes line trails off to the right. The date is Saturday 13 June 1998.

Opposite upper: About 1971, B130 ambles into Limerick past Ennis Junction with a loose-coupled goods train from Ennis. The double track line leading to Killonan and Limerick Junction is to the right of the train. As can be seen, there is no connection here between the tracks of the two lines, as the actual junction itself had been removed as long ago as 1910. The covered wagon immediately behind the locomotive is of Great Northern Railway origin – one of a number built in the early 1950s at Dundalk Works. At this stage, these vehicles could easily be distinguished by the suffix 'N' to their running numbers. Also of interest is the British Railways Freightliner container on the flat wagon fourth from the engine.

Opposite lower: In 1925, the Electricity Supply Board commenced construction of a large hydro-electric power station at Ardnacrusha, about four miles from Limerick. The GSR built a long siding, 1¼ miles in length, into the plant as the construction work was nearing completion. On 1 September 1962 the IRRS operated a special train to the plant, headed by J15 class No 183. The leading carriage is a six-wheeled Third Class coach of Midland Great Western Railway origin, dating from the 1880s or 1890s. Two of this type are preserved at the Downpatrick and Co Down Railway, with another in the care of the Railway Preservation Society of Ireland. Another is on display outside a hotel in Clifden, Co Galway. The second vehicle in the train is a CIÉ 'tin van', some 70 years younger, followed by two standard CIÉ 'Park Royal' carriages, built in 1955. The last one is in the newly introduced 'black and tan' livery, seen on Irish carriages in various variations well into the twenty-first century. The Ardnacrusha line was in occasional use for some years afterwards, with wagons of scrap leaving from time to time. *(Oliver Doyle)*

Above: On 6 July 1987, 'A' class No 018 (formerly A18) approaches Cratloe en route to Ballina. The train is the laden oil and coal train from Foynes to the now-closed Asahi plant at Ballina. Foynes also appears to have seen its last freight trains, despite its port thriving. It will be noted that there is no logo on the front of the locomotive as was normal at the time – doubtless it had re-entered traffic after an overhaul before painting had been completed.

Opposite upper: The Railway Preservation Society of Ireland operates all-Ireland steam train excursions, generally originating from Belfast or Dublin. Each May, a three-day tour is undertaken, which is the highlight of the Irish railway preservation calendar. This can traverse any line on the national network. In this view, the RPSI's 'Cu-na-Mara' rail tour passes Cratloe station on 11 June 1977. The carriages, of 1950s origin, are ex-CIÉ, now in the RPSI's care, while the locomotive is one of the world's oldest operational main line steam locomotives. This is ex-Great Southern and Western Railway J15 class No 186, one of two surviving members of the class, which is still in use on RPSI trains almost half a century after the rest of the class, along with all other steam locomotives in the Republic, were withdrawn. The J15s were regular performers on the Limerick–Sligo route in steam days. By the time this picture was taken, Cratloe station had been a private house for 14 years.

Opposite lower: Against a brooding dark sky 'A' class loco 035 is pictured heading south at Sixmilebridge on 7 June 1987. The train is a Gaelic Athletic Association special heading for Limerick, en route to a Munster Hurling Championship Match in Killarney. The former passenger platform is now a lawn, the station having closed to the public in 1963, and the building itself is a private house. Beyond the platform, and to the right of the train, there was formerly a short goods bank and siding, the site of which is now heavily overgrown by bushes.

Above: On 5 March 1976, B191 has the Athenry to Limerick goods, and waits at Ballycar to cross the 1405 Limerick–Ballina passenger train.

Opposite upper: Also on 5 March 1976, B191 pulls forward with the goods train after the passenger train had passed. The open wagons on the train were due to be loaded with scrap at Ardnacrusha siding.

Opposite lower: On 15 June 2003, loco 124 heads a push-pull set on the 1710 Ennis–Limerick train. The locomotive is pushing from the rear of the train. The well kept shiny paint belies the fact that the locomotive is by now 42 years old. Newly relaid track is evident; ahead of the train old track panels have been set aside to the left of the line. This area was always prone to flooding and in 2007 the line was shut for several months as a result of this.

Above: Ardsollus and Quin station. This was closed in 1963 and is now a private house. As often on Irish railways, when a station was situated between two villages, it bore the names of both. Trew and Moy, in Co Tyrone, was another example, as is the current station of Rush and Lusk, in north Co Dublin. The picture was taken from the cab of a locomotive passing through in the 1970s.

Above: Northern Ireland Railways 80-class railcars often made forays deep into CIÉ/Irish Rail territory with special workings, especially for GAA fixtures. Here, No 91 leads a six-car set at Clarecastle on 28 February 1993. The train was en route from Newry to Ennis, as Down were playing Clare in a National League game. The 'Down men' had to make the long journey home with defeat ringing in their ears… After the train set down its passengers at Ennis, it travelled on to Limerick to be serviced and refuelled.

Opposite: 141-class locomotive No 172 with its train of two 'Craven' coaches and a 'BR' generator van is pictured at Clarecastle on the last day of August, 1996. Between 1977 and 1988 there were no passenger services at all over this route, but from then onwards a limited Limerick–Ennis local service of one or two trains a day was re-introduced. The town of Ennis may be seen in the background. The train is the 1350 Ennis–Limerick.

Above: 141-class loco No 159 at the Dublin end of Ennis station on 29 September 1994. The once extensive locomotive shed and water tower are in the background. The signal cabin is comparatively new, as will be seen, but it is mounted on the old base. The passenger station (on the right) is painted in the bright blue used by Iarnród Éireann in the 1990s. Behind the locomotive shed, out of sight, is the area formerly occupied by the terminus of the West Clare Railway, whose narrow gauge lines connected here with the main line system. Following the closure of the WCR in 1961, the area became a car park and bus depot. Fuel for the buses was brought in by rail for many years afterwards, and here the locomotive is pictured shunting a tank of fuel into the siding which was used for this purpose.

Opposite upper: Ennis station about 1972, showing cattle being loaded on the up passenger platform – the station's cattle pens having been removed some years before. At one time cattle traffic was a major part of the railway scene all over Ireland, and in Ennis a large cattle mart was situated next to the station. Here, it is its final throes – the last cattle trains in Ireland were those to Loughrea fair in Co Galway, which ceased to be carried by rail in November 1975. The fashions of the day are of interest – witness the farmer in his best brown suit, dressed up for Market Day. Three cattle wagons, now showing signs of wear and tear, are being loaded here, and will soon be attached to the goods train being assembled in the distance. In times past, most stations had dedicated loading platforms for cattle, with pens to contain them when they were being loaded or unloaded. The pens were usually heavy fencing made out of old railway sleepers or rail sections welded together.

Above: On a very hot summer Sunday, 14 July 2002, 121-class locomotive No 124 has just arrived from Limerick with the 1530 Limerick Junction–Ennis train. This train was designed to take a connection at the Junction from main line trains between Dublin and Cork, and travel to Limerick, where after reversing it continued to Ennis. The carriages are a three car push-pull set with a driving cab at the other end to avoid the necessity to run the locomotive round to the other end at the end of the journey. In the case of this locomotive, with a cab at one end only, it would have had to turn as well, and the turntable has long gone. These locomotives were the only diesels which did not have a cab at either end. When introduced in 1961 this did not create any operating difficulties, as turntables were plentiful. After the end of steam in 1962, turntables fell into disuse all over the country, and few are now operational. Thus, 121-class locomotives have in recent years usually operate in pairs, with cabs outermost to avoid the necessity to turn. Single use has therefore been rare for a long time, but in the case of trains like that pictured above, the necessity to turn is removed. Single 121s were regular performers on push-pull trains in the 1990s, both on this line and between Dundalk and Dublin. As 2006 dawned, only two of these locomotives (the above plus No 134) were in use – by then, at 45 years old, the oldest operating diesel locomotives in Ireland.

In the photograph, two girls (with backs to the photographer) sit on the side of the platform where trains of the 3ft gauge West Clare Railway departed for Kilkee and Kilrush. This line was closed in 1961, the last of Ireland's once-numerous public narrow gauge railways, and the only one to survive long enough to be entirely dieselised. The train will leave again at 1715 for Limerick, from where a connection will be made into the Dublin train.

Opposite upper: 141-class locomotive No 150 is pictured on 3 September 1985 with a maintenance train on the River Fergus Bridge, just north of Ennis. On the left is a well wagon on which a crane is mounted.

Opposite lower: On 14 February 1976, 189 pulls forward having detached from the 1115 Limerick–Ennis passenger train. It will run round to the other end before departing for Limerick again. This overall view of Ennis station shows how much has changed on the railway scene between the 1970s and the beginning of the new century. On the left, we see the new goods shed under construction – destined to have a much shorter life than its predecessor. A long line of goods wagons indicates the healthy level of traffic on offer, all conveyed in loose coupled four-wheeled wagons. Continuing towards the right, we see a pile of empty beer kegs awaiting onward transit to the Guinness Brewery in Dublin, with an old CIÉ-owned Bedford lorry behind them. In the 1960s and 70s, lorries such as this were a familiar sight making deliveries from railway stations. An assortment of wagons is parked in the left foreground – nearest to the camera, a four-wheeled open wagon (latterly used for sugar beet), a covered van, a 'Lancashire Flat' with empty Guinness kegs, another van and beet wagon, and three more flats. On the extreme left is a newly laid siding. The old container gantry, then due to be replaced by a new one, is in the far left background. The footbridge across the passenger platforms is in the standard grey colour scheme used from the late 1960s until the late 1980s. To the right of the train a double decker bus carries the short-lived biscuit-brown livery (Am I the only person who ever found this livery attractive? – Author). This bus would have been used on peak hour services between Limerick and Ennis. One wonders why, if CIÉ were well able to fill double decker buses along this route, they justified withdrawing the passenger train service just two months later? Another double decker in the older navy blue and cream livery may be seen in the distance, while two local single deckers, which are typical of the period, stand in the foreground.

Above: 181-class No 189 beside Ennis signal cabin. It is St Valentine's Day 1976, two months before passenger services between Limerick and Ballina ended, leaving the entire route without a single passenger train until a limited Ennis–Limerick service was reintroduced in 1988. The former West Clare Railway goods yard is to the left. On closure of the WCR in 1961, this is where most of its rolling stock was gathered prior to scrapping.

Opposite upper: A nine-car NIR 80-class railcar set pauses at Ennis, on 28 February 1993, having just offloaded a large contingent of GAA supporters from Newry, who are attending the Down v Clare game. Once everyone is off the train, it will set off for Limerick to be serviced and refuelled. On the right, we can see the guard's van at the rear of the 1645 Ennis–Limerick train. On the right, former West Clare Railway 3ft gauge locomotive No 5C is displayed on a plinth. This locomotive is now in the care of the short preserved stretch of the WCR at Moyasta Junction, between Kilkee and Kilrush. While the locomotive was displayed here, it was initially situated to the right of the photograph, but later moved to this position, alongside the platform where it must have awaited departure many a time. On the left, much evidence of fertiliser traffic is to be seen.

Opposite lower: A pair of 121-class locos (122 and 124) await departure from Ennis for Limerick. 124, in the older livery, had failed and 122 was sent to the rescue. It will be seen that the track on the up line has a fair covering of weeds. It was little used at this time. The date is about 1973.

Above: Appearances of Mk 2 carriages were rare on the Limerick–Sligo route, but one exception was a Knock pilgrimage special on 10 October 1976. Here, 185 hurries its train past the now demolished signal cabin at Crusheen en route to Claremorris.

Opposite upper: Apart from GAA specials, the main source of irregular passenger traffic after the line closed to normal passenger trains was pilgrimage specials to Claremorris, for Knock. On 10 October 1976, a heavy load of 12 carriages labours near Crusheen, headed by two 141-class locomotives. Twelve carriages over a steeply graded line such as this would have been too much for one of these light locomotives. The author cherishes memories of one, on loan to NIR, attempting to start nine coaches on level track near Belfast – it could be heard for miles around, and the smoke effects were spectacular! The train is of interest: behind the locomotives is a luggage van, and the second coach is an ambulance coach for those with wheelchairs. The passenger carriages are a mix of CIÉ 1950s 'laminates' and Park Royals, and a dining car is included. This train had come from Cork, via Limerick Junction and Limerick. The pig in the field is oblivious!

Opposite lower: The Railway Preservation Society of Ireland has operated occasional specials over the line for many years, using their preserved steam locomotives and carriages. On 6 June 1987 ex-Great Southern & Western Railway J15 No 184, one of two of these engines preserved, crosses the bridge near Crusheen, running tender first. On this occasion, the Ennis Arts Festival had hired the train from the RPSI to provide local steam train trips in the area.

Above: Here, on the same day, 184 passes through Tubber en route to Ennis. The old station house, closed to the public in 1963, is on the left. At one time there was a short siding for goods traffic on the right.

Opposite upper: The RPSI special passes over Main Street, Gort, Co Galway, 6 June 1987. Who remembers the red rear number plates, used from the late 1960s until the modern system of car registrations commenced in 1987? Prior to that, the second two letters on the plate denoted the county it was registered in. The red Toyota Starlet carries the registration mark 'FI', indicating its origins in Tipperary North, while the beige Ford Cortina is originally from Cork (IF), and the red camper van is Dublin-registered (ZG). In front of Mullins shop, the cream car is a visitor from Galway (ZM). Imperial measurements are still is use, as shown on the bridge restriction sign, which warns that the maximum height is 15ft and 10in (4.82m).

Opposite lower: On a very wet day in the late 1970s, 121-class locomotive B130 waits in the loop with the Claremorris to Limerick regular goods at Gort. The first van behind the locomotive has a wood-planked body – few such wagons were still in traffic by then. One of the last B101 class locomotives in traffic, No 107, heads away from the camera with an overload goods going the other way to Athenry from Limerick. The fourth wagon in this train appears to be the only loaded one – it has a load of bagged fertiliser covered by a tarpaulin.

Above: An overall view of Gort station, early 1970s. B181 has the Limerick to Claremorris goods. Containerisation is beginning to creep into the railway goods scene; a Bell Lines container may be seen at the end of the train, on the left. These wagons have been left on the main line, while the locomotive shunts the yard before resuming its journey. In the goods shed road, one van accompanies several laden wagons of sugar beet, once a very important traffic along the line, as well as elsewhere in Ireland. Despite the cramped space, large tonnages of beet were loaded here for onward transmission to Tuam Beet Factory. At the end of the platform nearest the camera is a small cattle pen, used for loading and unloading cattle wagons. On the right, the locomotive shunts other wagons. The second wagon behind the locomotive also contains beet.

Looking at what remains of this scene today, it is hard to imagine such activity so recently in the past.

Opposite upper: The train described previously on page 29 enters Gort station in the early 1970s. This view can be compared with a similar view on page 136 from April 2010.

Opposite lower: On 21 October 1980, 187 enters Gort station with the 1505 empty sugar beet wagons from Tuam. Immediately left of the locomotive a breach may be seen in the old platform. This was created long after the last passenger trains had left, in order to aid the unloading of bagged cement from wagons.

Above: 'A' class locomotive No 036 enters Gort with a train of empty cement wagons en route from Athenry to Castlemungret, the far side of Limerick. The signal cabin could do with a repaint, and the goods siding on the left badly needs to be sprayed with weedkiller. This view dates from 15 May 1982. Already elderly, the last examples of this locomotive class would soldier on until 1995.

Above: Kiltartan level crossing, between Gort and Ardrahan, about 1976. The picture is taken from the old road bridge, recently replaced by the level crossing shown. Nowadays, it would be more likely that a level crossing would be replaced by a bridge for 'health and safety' reasons! The train is the northbound goods, in the charge of B181. In the middle of the train are several wagons of sugar beet destined for Tuam Sugar Factory. *(David Carse)*

Opposite: A Knock Pilgrimage special powers through Ardrahan, en route from Limerick to Claremorris on 9 May 1976. The locomotives are both of the 181-class, and are only nine years old, but B181 carries the original 'black and tan' livery worn by the class, while 188 has been repainted in the new 'Supertrain' livery, introduced three years earlier. As locomotives were repainted into this new livery, they lost their power classification letter. Upon repainting, B181, for example, became 181. The carriages in the train are of interest, as mostly represent types long gone. The leading vehicle is a generator van with accommodation for the train guard, colloquially known as 'genny vans'. The second coach is an ambulance coach, converted to carry wheelchair bound pilgrims and medical equipment for the infirm. This particular ambulance coach has been rebuilt from a CIÉ 'Park Royal' coach, built in 1955. The other coaches are assorted varieties of CIÉ 'laminates', dating from the 1950s. One of these carriages, brake standard No 3223, is now preserved in working order on Ireland's only preserved standard gauge railway, the Downpatrick & Co Down Railway, at Downpatrick. The Railway Preservation Society of Ireland have several also – these are in use on steam train excursions in the greater Dublin area.

Opposite upper: On a 'soft' day in the early 1970s, B130 calls at Ardrahan with a southbound goods train. To the right, a lone wooden bodied wagon awaits a load of beet, and just ahead of it is a ramp up which lorries could reverse to tip into wagons. In the foreground the platform is raised for the same purpose. The locomotive is shunting the goods yard.

Opposite lower: Over thirty years later, on 7 September 2007, Ardrahan station is a scene of dereliction, seen from almost the same spot as in the previous picture. Its reawakening as part of the new Limerick–Galway route has yet to come.

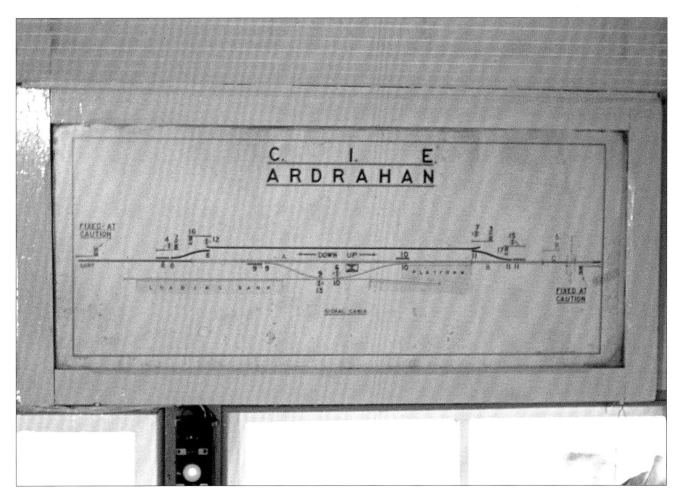

Above: Diagram inside Ardrahan Signal Cabin, 1976.

Opposite upper: On 20 October 1977, 173 heads a laden train of sugar beet through Ardrahan on the way to Tuam beet factory. On the left, several wagons await collection by a later train while a lorry loads beet into other wagons behind them. The train has halted while the man at the locomotive cab door delivers a message to the driver.

Opposite lower: The RPSI's preserved J15 class locomotive No 184 (Inchicore Works, 1880), drifts south with one of the Society's famous May weekend tours, on 15 May 1982 – two years after the locomotive's centenary. The leading carriage is of mid-1930s GSR 'Bredin' design. The location is Ardrahan.

Above: 'A' class No 017 brings empty cement wagons from Athenry to Castlemungret on 22 October 1980. The train is pictured near Craughwell.

Opposite upper: At Craughwell, on 24 October 1981, Driver Bobby Foster has locomotive No 190 on a laden beet train. The train is about to leave the siding on the right, leaving one empty wagon at the end to await filling. The photographer is facing Tuam, where the beet will go, but the train is heading in the other direction, ie towards the camera. This is because there was no loop at Craughwell, and the train will set off for Gort (behind photographer), where the locomotive will run round to the other end of the train and take it back the way it came, through Athenry, and onwards to Tuam. Over the whole beet campaign at this time, Craughwell station could be expected to load over 100 wagons of sugar beet.

Opposite lower: 141-class locomotive B177 departs from Craughwell with the daily Ballina–Limerick passenger train in the early 1970s. The train consists of a 1956-vintage CIÉ 'laminate' coach, a Park Royal coach, and a four-wheel luggage/guards van. On the right, a sleeper built loading bank can be seen on the goods platform. This ramp allowed lorries to reverse up to the edge and tip sugar beet directly into open wagons parked below. Such loading banks were to be seen in country stations all over the CIÉ system at one time. The signal box, no longer in use, has been demolished. The dark blue mini car on the right belongs to the photographer, and was just as familiar a sight at many Irish railway stations!

Above: North of Craughwell, at a site used for loading ballast for the regeneration work on the Western Rail Corridor, one of the few remaining 141-class locomotives (in 2007) heads up a ballast train which is being loaded on 7 September of that year. The ballast will be used on recently relaid track in the area.

Opposite upper: On 9 May 1976 a Knock Special heads past Craughwell, hauled by B167 (still in old livery) and a sister loco in the newer variation of it (post 1973). The neatness of the track is evident – this was typical even of lightly used lines at the time. On this day, four special trains of pilgrims traversed the line; one each from Cahir and Clonmel (shown), and two from Waterford.

Opposite lower: B168, on the daily 1355 Ballina to Limerick passenger train, leaving Athenry on 13 March 1976. On that date the passenger service had but weeks to go before withdrawal. The carriages are the usual pair of 'laminates', by then some 20 years old but destined for many more years in traffic. The rear coach is a very dirty 'BR generator van' – a rare visitor to this line at that time, as most of these vans were used on main line trains. The untidy scene in the foreground relates to alterations in the station layout – what was euphemistically referred to at the time as 'rationalisation'.

Right: Preserved J15 0-6-0 No 184 (built at Inchicore, 1880) passes 'A' class No 036 at Athenry. The steam train is part of one of the RPSI's famous 'May Tours' while 036 is parked beside the cement silo with wagons being unloaded. The date was 15 May 1982. The first two carriages, of GSR design, are of a type to be seen on service trains on the line up to about 1973.

Above: For an all too short period in the late 1980s/early 1990s, a preservation group named 'Westrail' operated steam excursions between Galway and Tuam, where they were based. They arranged for the total rebuild of ex-Great Southern and Western Railway J30 class 0-6-0T locomotive No 90. This small locomotive was originally built in 1875 for the Castleisland Railway Company in Co Kerry as the engine part of a passenger rail motor, but was rebuilt after a short time as a conventional locomotive. It gained its current appearance in 1915, after a major rebuild. Withdrawn in 1961, it escaped scrapping by being placed on a plinth as a display item – first at Fermoy, in Co Cork, and later at Mallow. Unfortunately, its forays on Westrail excursions were to prove short-lived, as a number of operational problems led to the cessation of these operations after a few years. In 2005, agreement was reached between Iarnród Éireann and the Downpatrick and Co Down Railway, as a result of which it was refurbished again at the RPSI works at Whitehead, Co Antrim, before taking up service on the DCDR's Downpatrick–Inch Abbey line in Co Down. It is now the oldest operational steam locomotive in Ireland, and one of the oldest in the world. Here, No 90 arrives in Athenry off the Tuam line on 10 August 1981 with a three coach train of Westrail coaches. These were preserved CIÉ 'laminates' of 1950s origin. The green livery preceded the 'black and tan' livery, seen on other coaches in these pages, but its authenticity was spoiled by the garish yellow paint on the ends, which was not authentic. None of these carriages have survived in working order.

Above: Loco 155 has arrived at Athenry with the laden cement train from Castlemungret, Co Limerick, 7 April 1990. Three years into the tenure of Irish Rail/Iarnród Éireann, the locomotive still carries the former CIÉ livery – much the same, but without the white stripes introduced by IÉ! Interestingly, while the loco still carries the CIÉ roundel on the front, it has also acquired the replacement Irish Rail logo on its side. Such variations were to be seen for a while in the late 80s and early 90s, echoing a time 30 years earlier when occasional CIÉ buses and railway stock could be seen with a new livery, but old logo, or the old livery with a new logo. The train will unload here, before returning empty. The impressive array of semaphore signals can be seen, as can a special train in the adjacent platform. This special train is described on page 45.

ATHENRY–GALWAY

We continue our journey over the next section to Galway. Although this is not part of the actual Limerick–Sligo route, we include it on account of the fact that modern passenger trains traverse the route from Limerick–Galway.

Above: 121-class locomotive No 132 departs from Athenry with the Athlone to Galway goods train, on 19 July 1976. Beyond the station, in the background, the line to Tuam is barely visible, sharply curving to the left. The main line to Athlone and Dublin stretches straight into the distance.

Opposite lower: Athenry, on the same date as the picture on page 43. A southbound empty coal/oil train, headed by loco 192, has reversed onto a siding in the background to allow passage for an enthusiast special train formed by Northern Ireland Railways stock. This consists of Mk 2 coaches, headed by NIR 'GM' locomotive 111. These locomotives were identical to the CIÉ 071-class, though delivered several years later. This train was en route from Dublin (Connolly) to Westport via Athlone, Athenry and Claremorris. It will be noted that loco 192 also carries the new IR logo but without white stripes as loco 155 on page 43.

Opposite upper: Freshly painted 121-class loco 132 shunts open wagons at Oranmore on 18 July 1976. The sidings on the left are adjacent to a scrapyard where the ex-Great Northern Railway diesel locomotive No 800 (later K801) ended its days, and on the right is the oil storage facility. The tank wagons in the siding there will be unloaded by having their contents pumped out via pipes to the storage tanks in the background. The locomotive was the Galway pilot engine, which used to leave Galway light, travel to Athenry, turn and come back (possibly with wagons from there if necessary), and shunt Oranmore as shown before returning to Galway. Of interest is the converted Scammell road lorry which was used by the private owners on the left to shunt the siding through the old goods shed, in which it may be seen sheltering.

Opposite lower: The approach to the once-busy Galway station, from the cab of a locomotive in the early 1970s. From left to right we see a very busy goods yard, with both container wagons and older four-wheel vans of varying origins. Immediately left of the signal cabin an old 'half cab' P-class bus is visible in the background. This was converted into a tow car. Semaphore signals watch over the proceedings as a pair of 141-class locomotives prepare to leave with the up day mail train for Dublin. On the right another 141-class locomotive awaits its next duty, while two more mail vans are parked in the bay platform beside it. The former Galway to Clifden line set off to the right of this locomotive, behind the water tower. The pointwork is a lot more complex than today, with a double slip in front of the signal box.

Above: Galway goods yard in happier and busier times, on 30 August 1999. Loco 084 has been newly painted, and heads a train of 23 four-wheeled timber trucks, which departed at 1355 for Waterford. On the right, 218 has the 1050 Galway–Dublin (Heuston) train, composed of the much lamented 'International' set of Mk 3 carriages, which became synonymous with this route. These carriages were considered by many to be the most comfortable passenger vehicles ever to run in Ireland.

Above: Galway, 1962. A brand new 121-class locomotive in original grey and yellow livery shunts goods wagons. Among these are two of ex-Great Northern Railway origin; the GNR had been divided bettwen CIÉ and the Ulster Transport Authority only five years earlier. In the background is a CIÉ tow truck formed from an old bus. This is in the then new red and cream livery, but with the pre-1962 'flying snail' logo on its side. To its right is a CIÉ lorry still in green – again with 'flying snail' on the cab door. At this time, vehicles in old liveries with new logos, and new liveries with old logos, were to be seen both on rail and road. The overall level of freight activity is in stark contrast with the scene at typical railway termini today, where no goods traffic at all is the general rule. *(Sam Carse)*

ATHENRY–CLAREMORRIS

This middle section of the route was opened in two stages: Athenry–Tuam on 27 September 1860, and Tuam–Claremorris on 30 April 1894. Tuam (approximately half way between the two towns) was one of the busiest locations on the route, and the northern terminus of the line for some 30 years.

Above: A busy scene at Athenry on 13 March 1976. At that stage and for many years previously, up and down Limerick–Sligo trains crossed here with up and down Dublin–Galway passenger and mail trains. This flurry of activity took place around 4pm each day. From left to right:

- the rear of the 1405 Limerick–Ballina train, hauled by 158 with two coaches, a four-wheel heating van and unusually trailing a bogie mail van.
- the 1305 Dublin (Heuston)–Galway hauled by 189 with an unusually light load for this service – four coaches and a 'Dutch' van (behind the engine). This was as a result of a recently upgraded timetable for this service, which gave a greater number of trains each day. In turn, this often resulted in fewer passengers per service.
- to its right the 1355 Ballina–Limerick consisting of B168, two 'laminate' coaches and a 'BR' van. Not in the picture, but present, is the 1540 Galway–Dublin (Heuston), which loaded to seven coaches and was hauled by B164. The middle train in the picture, in taking precedence, has caused the up Limerick and down Ballina trains to be shunted into sidings, while passengers remained on board. This practice would not be permitted under modern railway operating regulations.

Opposite upper: On the up side of the line between Athenry and Ballyglunin, a little known siding at Belleville was the source of a modest amount of sugar beet traffic. On 29 October 1975, locomotive 183 passes with a beet train. Empty wagons are parked in the siding and beet will be loaded by tractor shovel for collection by a later train. *(David Carse)*

Opposite lower: 'A' class locomotives, along with the 141 and 181-classes were regulars on the Limerick–Sligo line for much of the period between the end of steam in the early 1960s and the gradual abandonment of most of the route in the 1990s and early 2000s. In this view at Ballyglunin, on 28 November 1977, 045 with beet empties crosses 141-class No 173 with a laden beet train. The passenger platforms are beginning to become overgrown; it is some 18 months since passenger trains ceased. The empty train with 045 is the 1045 Tuam–Portarlington, and the laden train with 173 is the 0850 Limerick–Tuam.

Above: Two 141-class locomotives double-head the return leg of a Knock pilgrimage special heading north at Ballyglunin on 9 May 1976. The train had originated in Waterford. It is just one month after regular passenger trains ceased traversing the line and the platforms and track are still in good condition. Locomotive B171 still wears the 'black and tan' livery, but the second engine has been painted more recently, and wears the so-called 'Supertrain' livery of orange and black. The grey paintwork on the station woodwork was standard from the mid-1960s to the late 1980s. Ballyglunin is the station at which scenes for the 1953 film *The Quiet Man*, starring John Wayne and Maureen O'Hara, were filmed. In those days, the passenger train was a 60-class or 'D17' 4-4-0 locomotive, hauling a motley collection of old wooden bodied coaches in the CIÉ dark green livery of the day. Such locomotives were to be seen on the line until the end of the steam era in the early 1960s. *The Quiet Man*, at a quiet station – from the early 1960s until the end of passenger services in April 1976, just one train in each direction called here each day.

Opposite upper: The horses in the foreground pay little attention to one of the last timetabled workings along the line – the once-weekly Ballina–Foynes coal train which operated for a short while in the late 1990s. These trains appear to have been routed this way as it was the shortest way, and more efficient for crew rostering – or, was it a ploy to suggest the line was a viable operating railway? The truth was that no other traffic had been using the line for some time and after these trains ceased, nothing did again. Revival of the route is to be hoped for. The locomotive is a 141-class, the usual motive power on the line, and it heads through typical eastern Co Galway scenery on 19 July 1997.

Opposite lower: Tuam, looking towards Claremorris, in the early 1970s. This is a busy station scene, taken about 1972. On the left, there is evidence of brisk goods traffic with wagons parked at the platform. In the centre, we are looking at the rear of the northbound goods train, which is headed by an 'A' class locomotive. On the right we see B126 with the Ballina–Limerick passenger train, which consists of the usual two carriages and four-wheeled van. In the right background we can see new agricultural equipment unloaded on the platform, the goods store behind, and two CIÉ buses. One is an old P-class single decker which has had its engine removed. With CIÉ being responsible at the time for both road and rail passenger transport, it was by no means uncommon to see buses undergoing maintenance at railway stations. Immediately to the right of the locomotive cab, bags of fertiliser may be seen under the tarpaulin. The spire of Tuam Cathedral looms in the background.

Above: A freshly painted 172 heads for Athenry with an empty fertiliser train from Ballina on 12 April 1974. It is probably en route to Gouldings, Cork. On the left is the cattle market, and on the right is the Cathedral. The station, and Limerick direction, is behind the photographer.

Opposite upper: B130 at Tuam, 12 April 1974, with the Limerick–Claremorris goods train. The station is adorned with the standard grey and white paintwork of the period. Drab though this seems, it was much brighter than the dark green and cream which had preceded it for very many years, back to GSR days at least. These were the days: the station is well kept, and the goods traffic is busy and varied, judging by the size of the train and the assortment of different wagon types. It is to be regretted that in the early years of the twentieth century, rail freight of any sort has all but disappeared. The goods yard is in the top right of the picture.

Opposite lower: For an all too short few years in the late 1980s and early 90s, a preservation body named Westrail functioned in the area, operating diesel and steam excursion trains from their base at Tuam. Having acquired an 'E' class diesel from CIÉ, they operated the first privately owned main line diesel train in Ireland, and also restored ex-Great Southern & Western Railway No 90 to working order – thus also earning the accolade of having been the first preservation group to operate Ireland's oldest working steam locomotive. Here, Westrail's diesel, No E428, heads three Westrail-owned coaches at Tuam station on 19 August 1989. The view of the goods yard on the left behind the train contrasts with the image of it above – by now, it is weed grown and neglected.

Above: Loco 176 approaches Tuam from Claremorris, with the empty coal and oil train from Ballina to Limerick and Foynes. On this occasion, no oil wagons were on the train – it was coal empties only. By now (19 July 1997), the signal arm has gone, as Tuam cabin is switched out. The whole line from Claremorris to Athenry was one section by then.

Above: Westrail special with newly restored GSWR 0-6-0T No 90 at Tuam, 10 August 1991. The train has just arrived from Athenry and the photographer has been lucky in avoiding crowds of people in the picture, which is deceptive in this sense – the train was well loaded. This locomotive is now in the care of the Downpatrick & Co Down Railway, on its preserved line at Downpatrick.

Opposite: With only a fortnight to go until the passenger train service ends, black and tan liveried B168 is pictured here at Tuam with the 1355 Ballina–Limerick passenger train on 13 March 1976. As usual, the train has two carriages, but a 'BR' style generator van takes up the rear, rather than the usual four-wheeled guard's van.

Opposite upper: 'A' class locomotive No 010 (formerly A10) shunts empty wagons at Tuam on 29 October 1975. Laden wagons wait unloading on the left, while on the right are some wagons which are out of traffic awaiting repairs. This locomotive was destroyed in an accident in Lisburn Station, Co Antrim, in 1978 while hauling the Belfast–Dublin 'Enterprise' express train. As the train approached Lisburn station, an empty local passenger train was parked in its path, and it collided with it at speed. The driver was killed.

Opposite lower: Locomotive 122 heads past the beet factory sidings with the goods train for Claremorris, 3 December 1974. The fourth wagon in the train, painted in the older grey livery and with horizontal wood planked body, is of Great Southern Railways origin, and was one of a number designed by the co-author's grandfather in Inchicore's Drawing Office. The old Volkswagen 'Beetle' gives a nice period touch.

Above: 'A' class No 041 leads the Oranmore–North Wall oil train, which travelled via Athenry–Claremorris–Athlone–Mullingar. The photograph was taken on 17 August 1979 just north of Tuam sugar beet factory. A flat wagon travels behind the locomotive as a barrier between the driver and the wagons in case of fire. Another barrier wagon is at the back. It was unusual for flat wagons to be used as barriers – empty tank wagons or flats with containers placed permanently on them were more usual.

Opposite upper: Locomotive 122 at Milltown with the Limerick–Claremorris goods, 3 December 1974. A standard 'H' van is on the right – most goods trains were loose coupled in these times, and usually consisted mostly of covered vans of this type. Once a common sight all over Ireland, the standard four-wheeled goods van has now been extinct on the national railway system for many years. One is preserved, however, on the Downpatrick & Co Down Railway. The signal arm is down – the train is about to leave. On the subject of loose coupled goods trains, a retired driver from the area told the story of a famous goods train guard who was a regular on this line in the 1930s. He would regularly scrounge whatever food the locomotive crew might have brought with them, but never gave anything back, and was not known for his generosity. One time, the driver and fireman invited him to share their lunch on the locomotive footplate, and tried a large packet full of bacon for him, which he consumed eagerly. When the train arrived in Athenry, he had been very ill and was the colour of chalk! The crew had given him rotten rashers to teach him a lesson about stinginess, and he never bothered them for food again!

Opposite lower: Another view of 122 and train awaiting departure from Milltown.

Above: Westrail 'Orange Blossom Special' train for the country and western singing star, 'Boxcar Willie', on 22 June 1986. Westrail had acquired a number of carriages from CIÉ, almost all of 1950s 'laminate' design. The first two have been repainted in WR's attractive but short lived red and cream livery, but the other two are still in CIÉ livery. The locomotive also received a maroon livery for a time. The carriages are a mixed bag, which would hardly pass muster with modern health and safety regulations: the second last looks distinctly lopsided, and eyewitnesses said it travelled like this throughout its journey! The 'E' class locomotive in use here now rests at Dunsandle, Co Galway. It is not in working order at time the of writing.

Opposite upper: On 8 April 1995, what was almost certainly the last passenger train over the Athenry–Claremorris section comprised 10 carriages full of enthusiasts travelling on the Irish Traction Group's 'Freight Liner' railtour. The train left Dublin in charge of a brand new 201-class locomotive, but here 131 and 172 have taken over. The train is pictured near Milltown heading south on its return journey. In order to accommodate this railtour, the northbound coal and oil train from Foynes to Ballina was diverted via Athlone.

Opposite lower: Near Ballindine, 'A' class No 041 heads the Oranmore–North Wall oil train on 17 August 1979. The train came via Athenry and Claremorris, back down to Athlone, and into Dublin via Mullingar.

Above: 148 takes the Ballina–Limerick empty coal containers past Ballindine on 17 May 1997. Even at this late stage, the track hereabouts is well maintained.

Opposite upper: Ballindine, mid-1970s. The Limerick–Sligo goods passes through with B143 at the head. The former goods shed and platform (on the right) have long been disused and sold off. The former station house on the left had already become a private house following closure in 1963. *(David Carse)*

Opposite lower: A rare view of the short-lived Western Rail Corridor freight service taken at the Avenue Level Crossing, Claremorris, on 23 September 1994. The leading wagon appears to have containers of grain en route to Foynes. This is the 1545 Claremorris–Limerick train. It contains three Bell Line containers, one bogie flat wagon, and seven empty coal wagons from the now-closed Asahi plant in Ballina. These would also go to Foynes, the railway to which is now disused. As this train progressed, ten bulk cement wagons and another locomotive were added at Athenry for the final run into Limerick.

Above: Claremorris Southern Yard on 22 June 1974. The 1420 Limerick–Ballina train approaches Claremorris station, its single passenger coach and van headed by B128. The ex-Waterford, Limerick & Western Railway water tower remains.

Above: On 17 May 1997, locomotive 148 threads its way through the railway backwater which is the southern approach to Claremorris station. The limited clearance either side of the locomotive is evident here. The locomotive has arrived in order to collect the empty coal and oil wagons to return them to Limerick.

Opposite: Claremorris, 4 September 1962. On the left, a rather dirty 'C' class locomotive on the Sligo–Limerick train. After 1963, when the Claremorris–Collooney line was closed to passenger traffic, this train would have originated in Ballina instead of Sligo. 'A' class A14 has the Westport–Dublin train on the right. The carriages are of interest as they are of 'Bredin' design, built in Inchicore Works by the GSR in 1935. The second last coach is in the then brand new black and tan livery. The water columns on each platform are still in use and insulated against frost, as steam trains have not yet been entirely phased out. The green livery was used on these locomotives as well as passenger carriages, between the late 1950s and early 60s. The old MGWR footbridges and impressive array of semaphore signals will be noted. Despite more recent changes in both, the station building (which is behind A14 in this picture) retains its charm nowadays, having been well looked after over the years. *(John Langford)*

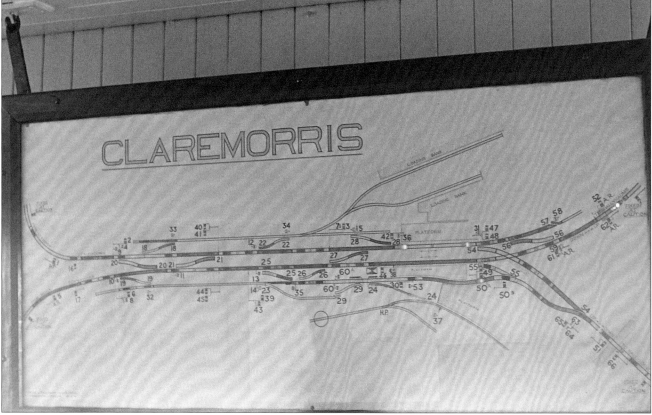

Opposite upper: Locomotive No 043 arrives in Claremorris with the empty coal and oil train on 15 June 1985. On the left another locomotive of the same class reposes. To the right of the train, over the tops of the wagons, the Ballina branch passenger train can be seen parked – this consists of a 'Laminate' standard and a BR Van.

Opposite lower: Track diagram in Claremorris cabin, June 1985.

Above: Following the end of all steam activity on the CIÉ system the previous year, a 'last fling' trip with steam was organised which covered much of the Irish railway network over several days in 1964. Here, the leading engine is No 130 of the Great Southern & Western's J15 class – regulars on what is now called the Western Rail Corridor. This trip was the forerunner of the legendary 'Three Day Tours' operated by the Railway Preservation Society of Ireland each May from the late 1960s to date – and which are now the highlight of Irish preserved railway activity, allowing several days of main line travel with main line steam locomotives. Indeed, one locomotive of the J15 class, 1879-built No 186, is a regular performer on such outings. Over the years, the RPSI has covered all sections of the Limerick–Sligo route at some stage or another. Here, the 1964 tour pauses in Claremorris. The train consists of a 'tin van', followed by two 1950s 'laminates', and then a pre-1920 dining car of GSWR origin. Next, another laminate, and bringing up the rear a truly ancient wooden bodied six-wheel brake van – but painted in the then new livery! *(John Langford)*

CLAREMORRIS–SLIGO

We now set out over the Claremorris–Sligo line. This stretch of the Western Rail Corridor (a modern name for the route) was known to generations of railwaymen as the 'Burma Road', in recognition of the fact that it was difficult to build (one contractor having bankrupted himself in the process) and the fact that the line went up hill and down dale – itself a reflection of how cheaply it had been constructed.

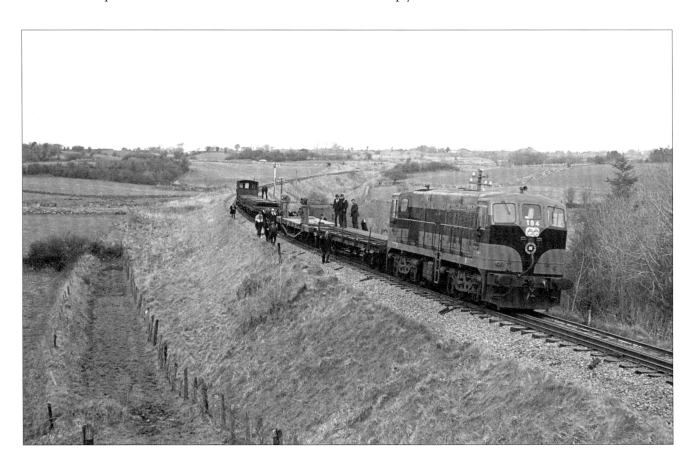

Above: In March 1975, the writing was already on the wall for the 'Burma Road', and sections of rail in reasonably good condition were lifted and exchanged with worn out rails from elsewhere. The good rails would therefore have further use after the final closure of this line, nine months later. Here, loco 184 has a rail train between Kiltimagh and Swinford while carrying out this work on 16 March 1975.

Opposite upper: The same train pauses in Kiltimagh station.

Opposite lower: In a very interesting move, on Saturday 24 September 1988, IR locomotive 052 hauled coaches 1460 and 1935 from Claremorris to Kiltimagh. The line was closed for 12 years but arrangements were made to bring the coaches here for the Kiltimagh Historical Society and the photograph shows them beside the goods store which will all form a museum. *(Joe St Ledger)*

Opposite upper: Classic 'Burma Road' view near Kiltimagh, early 1970s. An 'A' class locomotive heads north with a train consisting almost entirely of covered vans, though the second, third and fourth wagons are cattle trucks. The view is taken from the Guard's Van.

Opposite lower: In May 1975, the RPSI's May Tour visited the line for the only time. Here the train heads south towards Claremorris. The locomotive is No 186 – locomotives of this type were standard power on this line for many years. The carriages are all RPSI stock, the last one being the 'Rosslare Brake', a 66ft twelve-wheeler built by the GSWR with First, Second and Third Class accommodation, as well as a brake compartment.

Above: B145 receives the staff for the section to Kiltimagh at Swinford from the signalman (walking towards the loco cab). The train contains several covered vans, one open wagon, a cattle wagon and two modern containers on 20ft four-wheeled flat wagons. A covered van is inside the goods shed awaiting unloading, and in the distance behind the train can be seen an 'A' class locomotive. This heads the northbound goods for Sligo – the two trains having crossed paths here. The picture dates from about 1971.

Opposite upper and lower: Swinford, post closure in August 1993. The interior of station buildings was rarely photographed. While some 30 years had passed between closure to passengers in 1963, and the date of the photograph, the standard green and cream internal colour scheme used by CIÉ from the mid-1940s to late 1960s is shown clearly. Outside the track remains, but the weeds have taken over. *(J Beaumont)*

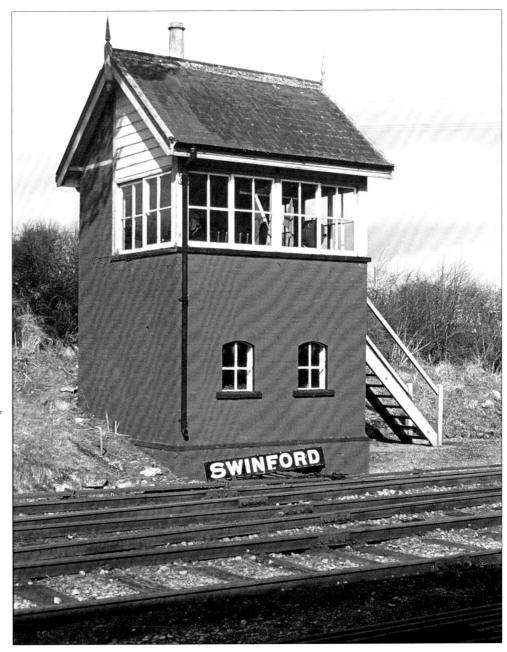

Right: Posed for the photographer (30 October 1975): one of the original enamel signs (of Waterford, Limerick & Western Railway pattern). This would have been removed years before and was obviously placed in storage.

Opposite upper: At the border of counties Mayo (to the left of the railway) and Sligo (to the right). This is Charlestown station (though on the Mayo side it is known as Bellaghy). A 'C' class locomotive heads a ballast train en route from Lecarrow to Sligo in 1968. On the right, a tractor may be seen – presumably with a trailer to unload from the wagon in the siding on the right. Passenger trains on this stretch had ceased running five years earlier.

Opposite lower: On the second last day of operation, 29 October 1975, B145 heads the Sligo-bound goods through Charlestown. There are still two wagons in the siding on the left – almost certainly the last wagons to be unloaded there, as the last train, hauled by the same locomotive, ran the following day.

Above: The southbound goods calls at Charlestown on 30 October 1975 – the last day the line was open for traffic. There is no hurry now, and there is no evidence of any goods being loaded or unloaded. Charlestown's goods siding and shed are empty, and the crane on the loading bank on the right is already rusty. Today, only the platform and track remain, the latter heavily overgrown and derelict.

Opposite upper: In May 1976, the 'Burma Road' is still in good condition, seven months after closure. For some years after it was closed, the line had an annual visit from the weedspraying train – the idea was that the line should not be hastily dismantled after closure in case of later uses being found for it. The locomotive is a rare visitor to this line – a B101 class locomotive, and by this stage one of the last of the class in traffic. The driver is Paddy Neville. Is the man at the left of the level crossing Count Dracula? The cars on the left are a cameo of these times: from left to right, a Morris Minor, a couple of Ford Escorts, a Vauxhall Victor (with red rear number plate), an Austin Cambridge (against the wall), and behind that a Ford Anglia. *(Richard Wall)*

Opposite lower: A view of the same location (Charlestown) in 2003, 35 years later. The station buildings have long gone, but the platform, the siding where the wagon was, and the main running line are still there. The rails may have been tarred over on the road, but a crack in the tarmac shows where one of the rails is not far below the surface.

Above: From the pages of a 'how not to' safety manual! The level crossing gates are shut to road traffic as the passage of a train is imminent, but this does not appear to concern the participants in a bicycle race. The picture was taken in 1975.

Opposite upper: The last train on the 'Burma Road' heads south near Tubbercurry on the 30 October 1975.

Opposite lower: At Curry, the RPSI May Tour in 1975 prepares to head north after a brief stop.

Above: The same train hurries away north of Curry, in the townland of Drumbawn. Loco 186 is in fine voice.

Opposite upper: Tubbercurry station, with the same RPSI train in attendance.

Opposite lower: In 2003, Tubbercurry station is a sad shadow of its former self. In the 28 years since the RPSI tour called, the platform shelter on the left has fallen down, and only the signal box remains – itself very derelict. On the right, the entire station building and goods yard has long been cleared away to make room for the town's ring road, just out of sight over the wall to the right. The water tower still stands at the other end of the station, out of sight in this picture. By 2007, even the signal box, by then unstable, had been cleared away. The rocks placed across the track bed are to prevent illegal access to the site.

Above: On 7 June 1961, the 1535 Limerick–Sligo is pictured at Tubbercurry. The railcars were of the AEC type, introduced on the line in the late 1950s to replace steam passenger trains on the through service, though steam remained on Tuam–Galway local trains. These railcars were the standard motive power on passenger services for a few years, before being replaced with diesel locomotive-hauled trains. The railcars have an old Third Class coach (probably of GSWR origin) as a centre coach, and the consist also contains a new four-wheel parcel van bringing up the rear. The group on the right at the lineside is a party of railway enthusiasts on an all-ireland IRRS/RCTS railtour (see page 85). On the left, cattle truck may be seen on the other side of the station. The photograph was taken from an adjoining field – the train was not really heading off into the grass! In 1963, through passenger trains between Limerick and Sligo had ceased, and Ballina had become he northern destination, with trains diverting from their traditional route at Claremorris, where they headed along the Westport line as far as Manulla Junction, and northwards from there to Ballina instead. *(J Edgington)*

Opposite upper: In happier times the up goods calls at Tubbercurry. Traffic is light, however. The locomotive is 'A' class No 018 and the picture was taken in autumn 1974. The following winter would see the line closed. *(David Carse)*

Opposite lower: 'A' class No 002 heads the Sligo–Limerick goods through Tubbercurry in summer 1974. The train includes a number of containers for the Bell Line en route to Waterford. On the right several covered vans await attention in the good yard over the wall – now the site of Tubbercurry's ring road.

Above: On 7 June 1961, one of several latter day steam excursion trains to visit the line pauses at Tubbercurry. The water tower on the right remains in place today. At this stage, steam locomotives were very rare visitors to the line; before two years more had passed, all steam hauled CIÉ service trains would be a memory, as would regular public passenger trains on this line. The locomotive is a J18 class 0-6-0 of Midland Great Western Railway origin, and the carriages are standard CIÉ 'laminates' of the day. *(J Edgington)*

Above: The annual weedspraying train which we saw in Charlestown has now progressed as far as Carrowmore. The name of this place is a mathematical impossibility: Ceathrú Mór (Carrowmore) means the 'large quarter'! Weedkiller can be seen spraying from the right hand side of the train. Having closed to passengers in 1963, the station still bears the old green and cream paintwork, and the siding adjacent to the goods shed on the right has long gone. *(Richard Wall)*

Opposite: Collooney, a small village where the 'Burma Road' met the MGWR's Dublin–Sligo line, had the luxury at one time of three railway stations. One was the main line station, still in use today; the other two were immediately north and south of it. Here, B145 descends from Carrignagat Junction (where the lines met) with the 1020 Limerick goods, and is about to enter the 'southern' station. The partially dismantled track to the right led under the main line (in the distance) to link up with the village's third station, which was on the Sligo, Leitrim & Northern Counties Railway's line. This line headed north east from here to Enniskillen and was closed in 1957. Thereafter, the line shown (known as the 'Southern Siding') was only occasionally used to store wagons.

Opposite upper: Coolaney had a small station a short distance from the village. In 2003, when this picture was taken, it was slumbering – as it still is. The station building is now a private house but the track remains in Irish Rail ownership. The rails can be made out under the tarmac on the road.

Opposite lower: RPSI No 186 powers through the former WLWR 'Southern Station' at Collooney, May 1975. This was the last steam excursion before the line closed. On the down platform the station sign is still of former WLWR origin – this would be a real collector's item today.

Above: The down afternoon Sligo train passes Carrignagat Junction in the late 1960s. This is composed of a three coach AEC railcar set, a type of train also to be seen on passenger trains on the Sligo–Limerick services for a time in the early 60s. On the right, the Limerick goods has arrived at the junction and waits in the shadows for the passage of the Dublin train before setting off on its last few miles into Sligo. The goods is headed by 'A' class No A55, now preserved in 'Hell's Kitchen' Bar and Railway Museum in Castlerea, Co Roscommon. *(Sam Carse)*

Opposite upper: Slightly off topic, but technically on the Limerick to Sligo route. At Ballysodare, between Collooney and Sligo, was Polloxfen's Mill which was rail served until the early 1970s. This rare photograph shows bulk grain wagons being loaded and unloaded, as well as the very intricate trackwork reflecting the cramped nature of the railway yard there. An AEC lorry is in the distance. The picture dates from 1968.

Opposite lower: Ex GSWR J15 class No 130 pauses at Ballysodare in June 1964 with a railway enthusiast's special train. A timeless scene apart from the newly introduced 'black and tan' livery on the elderly carriages. The station architecture here showed classic Midland Great Western design but today this scene is very different, as will be seen in the next illustration. The siding on the right leads into Polloxfen's Mill. *(John Edgington)*

Above: On 4 October 2003, 071-class No 072 powers through what is left of Ballysodare station with the 1200 Sligo Quay to Waterford laden timber train. This picture is taken looking in the opposite direction to the previous one. On the left of the train is the old goods loading bank and the former goods shed. Timber traffic from Sligo ended in December 2008.

Opposite upper: The 1415 Sligo–Dublin (Connolly) train leaves Sligo station on 12 August 1978 headed by a pair of 121-class locomotives. Almost every detail in this photograph has now gone: the 121-class locomotives, 'BR' type generator vans, 'Craven' coaches, mechanical signalling apparatus, and even some of the adjacent tracks. The goods brake van parked up on the right is another casualty of the passage of time and progress. The line curving away to the left is the short and steeply graded branch line to Sligo Quay, which has had no regular traffic since the end of 2008.

Opposite lower: Despite being used only for goods trains, the track was maintained in excellent condition on the Sligo Quay branch, seen here on 12 August 1978. Nos 161 and 155 struggle up the steep gradient with eighteen tank wagons and two barrier wagons. The train is the 1545 oil train from Sligo Quay to Dublin's North Wall yard. Loco 161 was removed at Mullingar and returned to Sligo with the Bell Liner train. The distinctive shape of Ben Bulben, on top of which Queen Maeve of Connaught is reputed to be buried, looms above the station, and the town.

Above: The very end of the 'Western Rail Corridor' route! On 12 May 1996, the Railway Preservation Society of Ireland operated its annual 'Three Day Tour' to Sligo. Former Dublin and South Eastern Railway 2-6-0 No 461 was the star of the show and is seen here at Sligo Quay for servicing. With wagons parked behind her, it looks as if she is about to set off with the up liner train – now THAT would have been a sight for sore eyes! Even well into the 1990s, Sligo Quay was still handling a considerable quantity of freight.

Above: On 18 April 1981, 037 has propelled a number of cement wagons onto Sligo Quay itself, in order to free up space in a very busy Sligo Quay goods yard that day. In addition to further cement wagons being unloaded there, trains carrying fertiliser and oil were also present, so storage space was at a premium.

Opposite: Overall view of the end of the line for passenger trains; Sligo passenger station, 15 June 1968. On the left, a goods train is stabled in the arrivals platform. A passenger carriage had been added to it to accommodate a party of railway enthusiasts on this day. On the next line, the left hand centre storage road, an AEC railcar set is stabled. These railcars were regulars on the Sligo–Limerick route in the late 1950s and early 1960s, but at this stage it is some five years since passenger services between Sligo and Claremorris have ceased, so this set will be used for a Dublin service. On the next siding, and on the right hand side (the departure platform), standard 1950s era 'laminate' coaching stock is stabled. An old Hillman car completes the scene on the right. Today, modern railcars dominate the scene and goods trains like this are a thing of the past, but the overall station building and canopies remain substantially as they were. There is now only one centre storage siding.

CLAREMORRIS–BALLINA

At this point, we revert to page 69, where we left Claremorris. The following pictures were taken on the route from there to Ballina and are included on account of the diversion of the Limerick passenger trains from Sligo to Ballina in 1963. Effectively, between then and 1976, when the through passenger train was discontinued, Ballina became the northern terminus – for passenger services – of the 'Western Rail Corridor'.

Above: Following rationalisation of the track layout in Claremorris station in 2003, the direct curve from the main up platform to the Athenry line was removed, leaving only a connection from Platform 3, as may be seen behind the locomotive here. On 5 August 2003, a timber train from Ballina to Waterford is headed by Northern Ireland Railways Loco No 112, which was on loan to Iarnród Éireann for some years at the time. Some of the semaphore signals have already been removed in connection with resignalling. The station looks very quiet in comparison with the scenes not too many years earlier on pilgrimage days!

Above: The 1355 Ballina to Limerick passenger train passes Manulla Junction on 15 March 1975. At this stage this station had not yet been reopened, as passengers changed between this and the Westport route at Claremorris. No 175 leads a motley collection of stock, as follows: first, the typical four-wheeled heating van, followed by a 1963-built 'Cravens' coach, a 1950s era 'Laminate' coach, and a 'BR' generator van. Bringing up the rear is a standard CIÉ bogie mail van. The likely explanation for this apparent surplus of non-passenger accommodation is that the rear coach had been worked out to Ballina carrying the morning's newspapers. The carriage of newspapers by rail was still commonplace at that time, often necessitating whole trains early in the morning on main routes. The left hand line leads to Westport.

Opposite upper: 'A' class locomotive 043 heads the 1400 Ballina to Foynes empty coal/oil train on 15 June 1985. With five coal wagons, followed by twelve oil wagons, then another five coal wagons, the load was already considerable before five empty bagged cement wagons were attached at Claremorris for onward transmission to Limerick. The train is pictured passing the long-closed station at Ballyvary, Co Mayo, which is now a private house.

Opposite lower: Locos 152 and 160 pause at Ballyvary on 3 May 1987. This was a test train which consisted of a Mk 3 set of carriages which certainly had a busy day. They had left Waterford very early that morning with a 'Knock Special' for Claremorris. While the pilgrims progressed (!) to Knock, the empty set was used to test clearances on the Ballina line before return to Waterford later that evening. The distinctive station architecture here was somewhat reminiscent of that used at Mallaranny, on the erstwhile Westport–Achill line by the Midland Great Western Railway Company.

Above: An RPSI special headed by ex-Dublin & South Eastern locomotive No 461 hurries past Straide, Co Mayo with the annual 'Three Day Tour' on 10 May 1992. The third and fifth carriages are in their original 1963 livery, maintained well into the 90s, while the others have acquired the post-1987 Irish Rail variation of the livery. The carriages were then hired from Irish Rail, though the Society now owns a rake of its own. The rear vehicle is a 'Dutch Van'.

Opposite upper: Loco 150 heads past Pollagh level crossing, between Straide and the River Moy bridge, on 30 August 1997. The train is the 1620 from Manulla Junction to Ballina. With no run round facilities at the newly reopened Manulla, the train had to unload its passengers there and continue to Claremorris to run round. It would then run empty back to Manulla before picking up its passengers for Foxford and Ballina from the Westport train. The branch set may look short – two 'Craven' coaches and a van, but all too often it consisted of a single coach and a van.

Opposite lower: In 1963, the Limerick to Sligo train was diverted at Claremorris, running instead to Ballina until that through service was discontinued in 1976. From then the service consisted of Claremorris (only) to Ballina, running in the path of the old Limerick train. Thus, this illustration may be seen as the tail end of the 'old order' on the western route, as far as passenger trains were concerned! The train is the 1144 Claremorris to Ballina, consisting of 'A' class locomotive 038, a 'Dutch' van and a Park Royal carriage. The train has slowed, as at that time there were severe speed restrictions here at the River Moy bridge. The date was 2 April 1988. This view must give an idea of what the Clifden or Achill branch lines would have looked like had they survived in use to the present day!

Above: Easter Saturday, 3 April 1988. The same train as above heads through Foxford towards Ballina with the morning passenger train. The train will leave Ballina again at about 1315 for Claremorris. The disused water tower on the right is of interest as it is unusually small and has a small outbuilding attached. On the left is the former goods shed. Foxford station had been closed in 1963, and in this picture had not yet been reopened.

Opposite upper: Foxford station on 28 January 1989, now reopened. The train is the 1315 from Ballina with loco 189, a single 'Park Royal' coach and a 'BR' van.

Opposite lower: Another shot reminiscent of what some former branch lines in the west would have looked like in more modern times. On 2 April 1988, 038 leads the 1315 Ballina to Claremorris train just north of Foxford.

Above: On 22 June 1974, 055 prepares to leave Ballina station with the afternoon train for Limerick. It will take some four hours for the train to reach there, via Claremorris, Tuam, Athenry and Ennis. The footbridge in the background was taken away once the picturesque down platform (left) was removed, for use elsewhere.

Opposite upper: Now-preserved 'A' class loco 055 pauses at Ballina on the same date as the previous shot. This scene was shortly to become unrecognisable, with everything left of the locomotive cleared away. The old steam facilities remain on the left in pre-1963 CIÉ green paintwork. There is much evidence of goods traffic on the right – nowadays it is all in containers. The branch goods brake van may be seen hiding behind the classic MGWR design signal cabin.

Opposite lower: Ballina station, winter 1974/5. The 'Rail Development Plan' for modernising the whole network has commenced with the removal of the entire west (left) side of Ballina station in order to make way for construction of the new bulk container-orientated goods yard. The old signal cabin is visible in the distance, behind the overhead crane; soon it will be demolished. The new cabin, on the right has yet to be commissioned. The rail for the travelling crane is visible in the foreground. The train is the 1315 to Limerick, by now the only remaining southbound train of the day. It is headed by loco 148 and includes one 'Craven' coach, one 'Laminate' and several vans.

Above: A contrast to the picture on page 103. On 22 February 1975, the Limerick train awaits departure from Ballina, with no evidence of any passengers. When a railway operator provides but one or two trains per day on a route like the one from Ballina to Limerick, it is hardly surprising to see little use being made of it. The train, 183 with a 'Laminate' coach, a 'BR' generator van and a four-wheeled 'tin van' is fairly typical. Behind the train may be seen level crossing gates. Prior to 1930 the line continued to Killala, and there remain several sidings just north of the crossing.

TUAM SUGAR BEET FACTORY

In December 1925 the first site survey for a sugar factory was carried out by engineers at Carlow and one year later this private enterprise project was in production. The following years were very difficult for the fledging sugar beet industry in Ireland but the response from Sean Lemass, Minister for Industry & Commerce was that three more factories should be built. Dáil Éireann established Comhlucht Siuicre Éireann Teo (Irish Sugar Company), in 1933 and President Eamon de Valera cut the first sod of the one at Tuam on 24 November 1933. The previous day he had performed the same ceremony at Thurles. The Tuam Beet Factory was opened on December 1934. Another was established at Mallow.

From the transport point of view the annual 'campaign' (harvest) was a major operation and although vast quantities were brought by road the railway played a vital role in providing transport. Overall for the four factories the railway would bring in anything from 300–500,000 tons, depending on the weather or crop yield each year. At the factory the beet was 'tared', which meant removing any clay or other extraneous matter, and sugar content sampled on the wagons before being washed under pressure and processed through the factory. CIÉ handled about 33% of all beet, the Beet Hauliers' Association 40% and the remainder was carried by private hauliers. That was the situation in Tuam in 1976 when the average distance from farm to factory was 65 miles. It was much lower for the other three factories – Thurles 43 miles, Mallow 35 miles and Carlow 16.5 miles.

In 1934/35 Orenstein and Koppel of Berlin supplied three locomotives to each of the factories at Mallow, Thurles and Tuam. They were numbered 1 to 3 at each factory (rather than a possibly more logical 1-9!) and were painted black with yellow lining. None were allocated to Carlow factory; the shunting duties there were performed by a vertical boilered locomotive built by John Cockerill of Belgium. Between 1948 and 1956 Ruston & Hornsby of Grantham, UK, delivered six diesel locos – two to Carlow, two to Tuam and one each to Mallow and Thurles.

Details of all these locos are listed in separate tables on pages 110 and 111.

We reproduce an extract from a beet circular issued by CIÉ for the 1962/63 campaign, showing specials mainly from Co Galway. As can be seen some were still worked by steam, this being the last season for such haulage as steam locomotives finished completely on 31 March 1963. The circular lists the various stations served and the daily Quota from 16 October 1962. Ardrahan and Tullamore each loaded 38 wagons, followed by Portarlington and Geashill. Over towards the east of the country, stations like Enfield, Castletown and Moate feature whilst the regular goods trains on the Ballina, Loughrea and Banagher branches catered for the beet traffic there. The last page shows stations from where beet would occasionally originate. It is interesting to note from this book's point of view that nearly every station from Sixmilebridge to Ballysodare would load beet. Tuam also received beet from 'Meath Road' stations like Wilkinstown and Drumree. We have already mentioned Enfield but there was beet from stations at places like Kilcock, Maynooth, Hill of Down and Mullingar. By special arrangement, beet was also loaded at Edenderry and Carbury.

From an early stage there was continual discussion about EEC Quotas for sugar which from Ireland's point of view were controversial. It became obvious that things would change. In 1984 Tuam closed and a few years later Thurles followed. It appeared that the sugar company would concentrate on Carlow and Mallow. Carlow, which had not been served by rail for many years closed and finally Mallow closed in 2006 thus ending 80 years of sugar production.

CÓRAS IOMPAIR ÉIREANN

BEET TRAFFIC—TUAM FACTORY

SEASON 1962/63

PROGRAMME

The following Time Table for the running of Special Trains to and from Tuam daily will operate from the dates mentioned hereunder until further notice.

The figures in brackets denote the number of laden wagons to be attached or empty wagons to be detached.

Spl. B.T. 63

ARDRAHAN TO TUAM
(Laden)

Commencing, 13th Oct., 1962

		Steam	
		Arr.	Dep.
		p.m.	p.m.
Ardrahan	(23)	—	1 45
Craughwell	..	pass	2 02
Athenry ..	..	2 19(a)	2 40
Ballyglunin	..	3 10(b)	3 49
Tuam ..	..	pass(c)	4 09
Tuam B.S.	..	4 20	—

(a) Cross B.T. 70.
(b) Cross 3.35 p.m. Passenger.
(c) Cross 7.05 a.m. Goods.

Spl. B.T. 64

TUAM TO ARDRAHAN
(Empty)

Commencing, 13th Oct., 1962

		Steam	
		Arr.	Dep.
		a.m.	a.m.
Tuam B.S.	..	—	9 30
Tuam ..	..	pass	9 40
Ballyglunin	..	pass(a)	10 00
Athenry ..	(1)	10 33	11 00
Ardrahan	(16)	11 35	—

(a) Cross 3.40 a.m. Goods which will shunt at Ballyglunin and arrive Tuam 10.24 a.m.

One wagon for Belville to go by Goods from Athenry.

Spl. B.T. 65

ENNIS TO TUAM
(Laden)

Commencing, 13th Oct., 1962

		Steam	
		Arr.	Dep.
		p.m.	p.m.
Ennis	..	— (a)	4 55
Tubber ..	(1)	5 33	5 50
Gort ..	(11)	6 07	6 30
Ardrahan ..	(11)	6 53(b)	7 30
Craughwell	..	pass	7 47
Athenry ..	..	8 04	8 20
Tuam ..	..	pass	9 10
Tuam B.S.	..	9 20	—

(a) Cross 6.45 a.m. Goods.
(b) Cross 7.05 a.m. Goods.

Spl. B.T. 66.

TUAM TO ENNIS
(Empty)

Commencing, 13th Oct., 1962

		Steam	
		Arr.	Dep.
		a.m.	p.m.
Tuam B.S.	..	—	11 30
Tuam ..	..	pass	11 40
			a.m.
Ballyglunin	..	12 04(a)	12 13
Athenry ..	(5)	12 46	1 15
Ardrahan ..	(16)	1 50	2 10
Gort ..	(11)	2 31	2 51
Tubber ..	(1)	3 08	3 20
Ennis ..	(1)	3 55	—

(a) Cross B.T. 71.

Spl. B.T. 67

ARDRAHAN TO TUAM
(Laden)

Commencing, 13th Oct., 1962

		Diesel Arr. a.m.	Dep. a.m.
Ardrahan	(4)	—	6 10
Craughwell	(9)	6 29	6 49
Athenry ..	..	7 06(a)	7 25
Ballyglunin	..	7 53(b)	8 31
Tuam B.S.	..	9 00	—

(a) Cross 4.20 a.m. Goods.

(b) Cross 7.55 a.m. pass and 6.45 a.m. goods.

Athenry attach four wagons off B.T. 73 and any other overload

Spl. B.T. 68

TUAM TO ARDRAHAN
(Empty)

Commencing, 13th Oct., 1962

		Diesel Arr. a.m.	Dep. a.m.
Tuam B.S.	..	—	3 45
Ballyglunin	..	pass (b)	4 14
Athenry ..	(6)	4 40	4 52
Craughwell	(9)	5 00	5 24
Ardrahan	(6)	5 45	—

(b) Cross B.T. 75.

Spl. B.T. 69

PORTARLINGTON TO TUAM
(Laden)

Commencing, 13th Oct., 1962

		Diesel Arr. p.m.	Dep. p.m.
Portarlington	(8)	—	2 20
Geashill ..	(9)	2 44	3 00
Tullamore ..	(13)	3 18	3 50
Clara ..	..	pass	4 05
Ballycumber	..	4 14(b)	5 08
Athlone ..	..	5 37(c)	6 10
Carrowduff	..	pass	6 30
Ballinasloe	..	pass	6 44
Woodlawn	..	pass(d)	7 11
Athenry ..	..	7 36	7 50
Tuam B.S.	..	8 45	—

(b) Cross 4.45 p.m. Pass.
(c) Cross B.T. 70 and 5.45 p.m. Goods.
(d) Cross 4.35 p.m. Goods which will depart Woodlawn at 7.13 p.m. and arrive Ballinasloe at 7.35 p.m.

Athlone detach 6 laden off B.T. 69 and attach to B.T. 71.

Detach one at Athenry for B.T. 77.

Spl. B.T. 70

TUAM TO PORTARLINGTON
(Empty)

Commencing, 13th Oct., 1962

		Diesel Arr. p.m.	Dep. p.m.
Tuam B.S.	..	—	1 05
Ballyglunin	..	pass	1 34
Athenry ..	..	2 00(e)	2 55
Ballinasloe	..	pass	3 44
Carrowduff	..	pass	4 00
Athlone ..	..	4 16(h)	11 15
Clara ..	..	12 05(f)	12 19
Tullamore	(20)	12 42	1 00
Portarlington	(8)	1 50 a.m.	—

(e) Cross B.T. 63 and 12.45 p.m. Pass.
(f) Cross B.T. 75.
(h) Cross B.T. 73.

L.E. Portarlington to Athlone at 2.00 a.m. (to work 8.55 a.m. Pass) or working overload.

Spl. B.T. 71 TULLAMORE TO TUAM (Laden) Commencing, 13th Oct., 1962 Diesel*			
		Arr. p.m.	Dep. p.m.
Tullamore	(18)	—	6 30
Clara ..	(6)	6 52(a)	8 35
Ballycumber	(4)	8 46	9 05
Athlone East	(6)	9 39	10 06
Athlone ..	..	pass(b)	10 10
Ballinasloe	..	pass	10 42
Woodlawn	..	pass(c)	11 09
Attymon ..	..	pass	11 20
Athenry ..	..	11 34	11 45
Ballyglunin	..	pass(d)	12 11
Tuam B.S.	..	12 40a.m.	—

(a) Shunt for 6.47 p.m. Passenger,
6.50 p.m. Passenger and cross
B.T. 74.
(b) Cross 8.15 p.m. Mail.
(c) Cross 8.35 p.m. Goods.
(d) Cross B.T. 66.
Athlone to attach six wagons off

Spl. B.T. 72 TUAM TO TULLAMORE via CLAREMORRIS (Empty) Commencing, 13th Oct., 1962			
		Arr. p.m.	Dep. p m
		Diesel	
Tuam B.S.	..	—	9 40
Claremorris	..	10 29(a)	10 45
Castlerea ..	..	11 46(b)	12 20
Ballymoe ..	..	pass	12 33
Donamon ..	..	pass	12 44
Roscommon ..	..	pass	12 57
Kiltoom ..	..	pass	1 23
Athlone ..	(6)	1 40(c)	—
		a.m.	a.m.
Athlone ..			2 00
Clara ..	(20)	2 38	3 00
Tullamore	(8)	3 17	—

(a) Cross 9.05 p.m. Passenger.
(b) Cross 11 05. p.m. Mail.
(c) Cross 8.35 p.m. Goods and 8.20
p.m. Goods.
Clara send 14 empties to Branch

Above: Two of the steam locomotives used by CSET have survived into preservation, and have been restored for use on Ireland's only full-size heritage railway line, the Downpatrick & Co Down Railway. Here, former Mallow Beet Factory No 3 (built 1935) awaits departure from Downpatrick to Inch Abbey on a summer Sunday afternoon in 2005. The journey is 3km long and features steam haulage and vintage coaching stock, some of the carriages in daily use being over 100 years old. The railway is also home to Thurles factory's No 1. None of Tuam's three locomotives survive. *(J Beaumont)*

TUAM FACTORY—PROGRAMME

STATION	Daily Quota from 16th Oct., 1962	Service for Laden and Empty Wagons	
		Empty wagons to be supplied from Tuam Beet Siding, unless otherwise stated	
		Laden Wagons	Empty Wagons
Ballycar	2	Goods	Limerick Supply.
Ennis (West Clare)	1	,,	Bt. 66.
†Tubber	1	Bt. 65	Bt. 66.
†Gort	11	Bt. 65.	Bt. 66.
†Ardrahan	38	B.T. 63, 65, 67	B.T. 64, 65, 66
Craughwell	9	B.T. 67	B.T. 68
Athenry	7	B.T. 67	B.T. 66 and B.T. 68
Oranmore	2	B.T. 67	Galway Supply
Belville	1	Goods	B.T. 64 and Goods
Enfield	5	B.T. 72	5.45 a.m. Goods and 4.35 p.m. Goods
Castletown	5	B.T. 77	B.T. 70 and B.T. 74
Moate	1	5.15 a.m. Goods and B.T. 77	B.T. 78
Streamstown	1	5.15 a.m. Goods and B.T. 77	B.T. 78
†Portarlington	19	B.T. 69, 73	B.T. 70 and B.T. 74
†Geashill	19	B.T. 69, 73	B.T. 70 and B.T. 74
†Tullamore	38	B.T. 69, B.T. 71, B.T. 73	B.T. 70 and B.T. 72
Banagher	4	Goods and B.T. 75	B.T. 72 and Goods
Belmont	5	Goods and B.T. 75	B.T. 72 and Goods
Ferbane	5	Goods and B.T. 75	B.T. 72 and Goods
†Clara	6	B.T. 71	B.T. 72
†Ballycumber	4	B.T. 71	B.T. 74
Athlone	1	B.T. 77	B.T. 72 and B.T. 78
Ballinasloe	13	B.T. 77	B.T. 78
Dunsandle	1	B.T. 75 and Goods	B.T. 78 and Goods
Loughrea	9	B.T. 75 and Goods	B.T. 78 and Goods
Ballina	3	Goods	Inwards Discharge
TOTAL	213 (Including 2 ex Ballyvary, etc.		

† Loading starts at these stations on 13th October, 1962.

Comhlucht Siuicre Éireann Teo – STEAM LOCOMOTIVES

Builders:	Orenstein & Koppel, Berlin
Wheel Arrangement:	0-4-OT
Cylinders:	11⁷⁄₁₆ in × 15¾ in
Wheels:	2ft 7½in diameter
Wheelbase:	5ft 11in
Boiler Pressure:	176 psi
Water:	400 gallons
Weight:	19 tons 14 cwt
Haulage:	285 tons on level, 116 tons on 1/100, 68 tons on 1/50

No	Works No	Year	Factory
1	12473	1934	Mallow
2	12474	1934	Mallow
3	12662	1935	Mallow *
1	12478	1934	Tuam
2	12477	1934	Tuam
3	12664	1935	Tuam
1	12475	1934	Thurles *
2	12476	1934	Thurles
3	12663	1935	Thurles

Preserved at Downpatrick & Co Down Railway

Commencing dates and quotas to be advised in respect of the following stations :—

Sixmilebridge	Ballymoe	Drumree	Maynooth
Clarecastle	Dunsandle	Ballyhaunis	Killucan
Ennis	†Donamon	†Charlestown	Mullingar
Crusheen	Ballinlough	Wilkinstown	Newtownforbes
Ardsollus	†Claremorris	Fairyhouse	Multyfranham
†Ballindine	†Ballyvary	†Milltown	Mostrim
†Kiltimagh	†Castlebar	Athlone	Attymon
†Ballysodare	Kilmessan	Ballyglunin	Longford
Knochcrogery	Bective	Kilcock	Woodlawn
†Roscommon		Hill of Down	†Swinford
†Balla			†Castlerea

†Two wagons daily ex these stations commencing with two at Ballyvary on **16th Oct., 1962.**

Loading at Edenderry and Carbury will commence on 26th November and be worked by special arrangement.

The Beet must in all cases be loaded in Open Trucks.

Everything possible must be done to release the inwards laden Trucks promptly to assist in meeting demands for Beet Traffic. Stations must wire Rail Control Officer and Inspector Coughlan at Tuam early each day the number of Open Trucks available from inwards discharge to meet next day's Beet loading, so that Specials conveying empty wagons may be reduced accordingly and the spare trucks utilised to best advantage elsewhere. THIS INSTRUCTION MUST RECEIVE THE STATION MASTER'S PERSONAL ATTENTION.

The Quotas must not be altered in any circumstances without the authority of the Rail Control Officer.

BY ORDER.

Amiens St. Station,
Dublin, October, 1962.

Comhlucht Siuicre Éireann Teo – DIESEL LOCOMOTIVES

Builders:	Ruston & Hornsby, Grantham
Wheel Arrangement:	4 wheel
Wheels:	3ft diameter
Wheelbase:	5ft 9½in
Length:	20ft 6½in
Weight:	17 tons

BHP: 80/88
RPM: 1000

Engine:
Ruston Mark 4VPHL vertical cold starting oil engine – 4 cylinder.
Direct coupled engine by a flexible coupling to gearbox.
Drive from gearbox to axles is by duplex roller chains.

No	Works No.	Year	Factory
-	252843	1948	Carlow
-	305322	1951	Mallow
-	312424	1951	Thurles
-	312425	1951	Tuam
-	382827	1955	Carlow
-	395302	1956	Tuam

Opposite upper and lower: Tuam Beet Factory Siding, 29 October 1975. For many years, the sugar factories at Tuam, Mallow, Carlow and Thurles provided very heavy seasonal traffic for CIÉ. Huge tonnages of this root crop were loaded at stations all over the midlands, south and south west of Ireland for onward transit to the nearest factory. None remain today. Tuam factory commenced operations in 1934 and closed completely in 1983. As will be seen in the next few photographs, the facilities provided were considerable, so much so that Comhlucht Siuicre Éireann Teo (CSET) had their own fleet of locomotives – first steam, latterly diesel. With industrial private-owner locomotives being a rarity in Ireland, it is of interest that several CSET locomotives are now preserved. Here, a CSET-owned Ruston diesel locomotive shunts empty beet wagons. The rudimentary nature of some of the track work is evident – the curve on the left seems to be made of a number of short straight sections, rather than a smooth curve – but such was quite satisfactory for an industrial site! There were three of these diesel locos, one each at Tuam, Mallow and Carlow. All survive; the Carlow one has been returned to working order, based at the Railway Preservation Society of Ireland's steam locomotive works at Whitehead, Co Antrim. Two of the nine steam locomotives owned by CSET have survived; both are owned by the Downpatrick & Co Down Railway, on which line one may be regularly seen in use.

Above: An overall view of the beet factory sidings, 29 October 1975, taken from up a signal post – a favourite 'trade-mark' vantage point of the co-author's brother, who took this view. There are eight parallel roads. In the middle is one train of laden beet which had just arrived. Either side, empty wagons abound; these will be marshalled into trains and sent all over the country to be reloaded, picked up, and brought back. The beet season, known on the railway as the 'beet campaign', stretched from late autumn each year into the following January. The main line is the extreme left hand track – it is clearly still well cared for at this stage, but only six months will elapse before passenger trains past here will cease. Locomotive 183, not yet ten years old, is in attendance. *(David Carse)*

KNOCK SPECIALS

Claremorris station has for many years been synonymous with Knock Pilgrimage Specials. The story of Knock began on 21 August 1879 when an apparition of the Virgin Mary, St Joseph and St John the Evangelist was reported by fifteen witnesses at the south gable of Knock Parish Church. Over the years, Knock has grown into a major pilgrimage centre, and is recognised as Ireland's national Marian Shrine. One and a half million pilgrims visit annually, the bulk now travelling by coach. But it was not always thus. Until the 1920s the number of visitors from outside the immediate area was small, and were catered for by service trains which served Ballyhaunis, as well as Claremorris. However, Claremorris is closer to Knock, and traffic of this nature to Ballyhaunis station never developed beyond a trickle. The first recorded special pilgrimage train to Claremorris was on 18 August 1929, when two trains operated on behalf of the St Vincent de Paul Society, from Dublin's Broadstone station. Following the foundation of the Knock Shrine Society in the early 1930s, organised trips from all over Ireland became more common, and traffic increased to unprecedented levels. For example, in 1936 there were 14 special trains, with 38 trains by 1940 carrying 7,568 passengers. Most of these trains operated between May and October each year. The next few photographs will show the heavy passenger traffic and complicated train operations on Knock Special days.

Above: On 11 October 1981, locos 176 and 142 bring ten Mk 2 coaches into Claremorris from Tralee, Co Kerry. The train had left at 0700, and arrived here at 1352, 42 minutes late. It is tempting to suggest that this six and three quarter hour pilgrim's progress all the way from the south west was penance enough! On the extreme left, buses line up to take the weary passengers for the few miles to Knock Shrine.

Above: The Tralee train has parked on the right, with the locomotives now switched to the other end in preparation for the return journey. In the meantime, 153 and 156 arrive with the 0820 special train from Waterford. This train loaded to ten Mk 2 coaches as well. Three other trains had come from the Limerick direction, in addition to three from the Dublin line (curving away to the left). These had originated in Dundalk, Newbridge and Athy.

Opposite upper: Most Knock Specials carried a carriage specially adapted for wheelchair users. Some were converted from 1950s Park Royal coaches, as seen here, by the addition of central double doors. To the left of this coach is Radio Studio coach RS23 – from these coaches commentaries could be given en route, and important announcements made. This picture dates from the late 1970s. *(David Carse)*

Opposite lower: During the afternoon, Claremorris station was a scene of great congestion, as up to 140 passenger coaches and up to 30 locomotives would be stabled here for the afternoon. Every available siding was used to accommodate these, and many were stored down the stub of the former Ballinrobe branch, which had closed in 1963. Here, on a wet day in the 1970s, we see a comparatively light day, with six locomotives in evidence. *(David Carse)*

Right: Awaiting departure in the evening: three specials, each headed by two locomotives, wait for their slot in the evening's busy timetable. Many passengers will have boarded their trains at 0700 and 0800 in the morning, and will not be home before midnight. *(David Carse)*

Opposite upper: Outside Claremorris station, large numbers would await pilgrims on pilgrimage days. Here at least eleven buses may be seen parked on the station approach road on one day in the late 1970s. *(David Carse)*

Opposite lower: A special train from the Athlone direction slows as it approaches journey's end on an unknown date in the 1970s. Locos 122 and 121 head a train of at least nine carriages, mostly of several 'Laminate' designs, but at with at least one 'Craven' coach behind the 24xx series dining car. *(David Carse)*

Above: B151 takes a breather from a Knock Special on the weed grown Ballinrobe siding. In the background, the station is clearly choked with carriages awaiting the evening departures to points all over Ireland. Behind the photographer, the line continues for a short way before a buffer stop marks the current end of the line. Prior to 1963, this was the start of the line to Ballinrobe. The daisies between the rails sway in the early summer sun – 23 June 1974 is a good day for railway photography.

Córas Iompair Éireann Working Time Table

26

Limerick to Ennis, Tuam and Sligo.

Distance from Limerick	UP TRAINS	WEEK-DAYS 1 Sectional Running Pas. D	Pas. S	Gds. D	Gds. S	2 Goods Loco. D.E. arr.	dep.	3 Pass. M. Loco. D.E. arr.	dep.	4 Goods Loco. D.E. arr.	dep.	5 Pass. M.* D.E. arr.	dep.	6 Pass. D.E. arr.	dep.	7 Pass. Loco. D.E. arr.	dep.	7a Pass D.E. arr.	dep.
Mls.						a.m.	a.m	p.m.	p.m.	a.m.	a.m.	p.m.	p.m.	p.m.	p.m.	p.m.	p.m.	p.m.	p.m.
—	**LIMERICK** W ¶ ●	**0**	**0**	**0**	**0**	...	**3 40**	...	...	...	**8 50**	...	**12 45**	...	**3 15**	...	...	...	...
	,, Check	...	...	...	...	...	...	...	...	...	...	...	...	...	...	...	...	...	...
4	LONGPAV'M'NT HALT + D ¶	6	7	11	12	...	3 53	...	...	...	9 03	...	12 52	C.	R.	...	...	...	...
9¾	CRATLOE HALT ...	9	10	15	18	...	4 08	...	...	...	9 18	C.	R.	C.	R.	...	...	...	...
13	SIXMILEBRIDGE HALT ...	4	4	6	7	...	4 14	...	...	9 26	9 35	1 10	1 11	3 40	3 41	...	...	...	...
16½	BALLYCAR HALT + ¶	5	6	8	11	...	4 22	...	...	9 47	9 57	1 18	1 19	3 48	3 49	...	...	...	...
19¾	ARDSOLLUS H ...	4	6	9	11	...	4 31	...	...	10 10	10 16	1 25	1 26	3 55	3 56	...	...	...	...
22¾	CLARECASTLE HALT ¶	4	5	8	10	...	4 39	...	...	10 28	10 55	1 32	1 33	4 02	4 03	...	...	...	...
24¾	**ENNIS** ...W ¶ ●	**3**	**3**	**5**	**5**	**4 46**	**5 30**	...	...	**11 04**	**2 05**	**1 38**	**1 45**	**4 08**	**4 15**	...	...	...	...
32½	CRUSHEEN HALT ¶	12	14	18	23	...	5 50	...	...	2 27	2 37	1 59	2 00	4 29	4 30	...	...	...	...
36¾	TUBBER HALT ...	5	6	10	11	...	6 00	...	...	2 51	2 56	2 07	2 08	4 37	4 38	...	...	...	...
42¼	GORT W ¶	7	8	13	13	6 15	6 30	...	...	3 13	3 33	2 17	2 19	4 47	4 49	...	...	...	...
49	ARDRAHAN ... + ¶	9	11	16	19	6 50	7 00	...	...	3 53	4 00	2 30	2 31	5 00	5 01	...	...	...	...
55	CRAUGHWELL HALT + ¶	8	10	15	15	...	7 17	...	...	4 19	4 26	2 41	2 42	5 11	5 12	...	...	...	...
60¼	**ATHENRY** D W ¶ ●	**7**	**9**	**15**	**15**	**7 34**	**9 17**	**12 02**	**12 13**	**4 45**	**6 00**	**2 51**	**3 00**	**5 21**	**5 26**	**6 47**	**7 03**	...	**10 00**
70	BALLYGLUNIN HALT ¶	13	15	24	26	C.	R.	12 28	12 30	6 28	6 33	To Galway		5 41	5 42	7 18	7 20	C.	R.
76	**TUAM** D W ¶ ●	**8**	**9**	**17**	**18**	**10 12**	**11 40**	**12 40**	...	**6 54**	**7 25**	...	...	**5 52**	**5 55**	**7 30**	...	**10 25**	...
80¾	CASTLEGROVE HALT	6	7	10	12	C.	R.	...	...	...	7 37	...	...	6 03	6 04	...	...	...	...
85	MILLTOWN (GALWAY) ¶	6	7	12	12	12 06	12 19	...	...	...	7 49	...	...	6 12	6 13	...	...	...	...
88¾	BALLINDINE HALT + ¶	6	6	10	10	12 33	12 49	...	...	...	7 59	...	...	6 21	6 22	...	...	...	...
93¼	**CLAREMORRIS** D W ¶ ●	**7**	**8**	**13**	**13**	**1 06**	**2 20**	...	...	**8 14**	...	...	...	**6 31**	**6 46**	...	...	...	...
102¾	KILTIMAGH ... ¶	13	21	26	30	2 50	3 26	...	...	...	...	...	...	7 01	7 03	...	...	...	...
110½	SWINFORD ... W ¶	10	15	20	20	3 50	4 21	...	...	...	...	...	...	7 15	7 17	...	...	...	...
117¼	CHARLESTOWN + ¶	10	15	19	21	4 44	5 02	...	...	...	...	...	...	7 29	7 30	...	...	...	...
120¼	CURRY HALT... N	4	8	11	12	C.	R.	...	...	...	...	...	...	7 36	7 37	...	...	...	...
124	TUBBERCURRY W ¶	6	9	12	12	5 34	5 59	...	...	...	...	...	...	7 45	7 47	...	...	...	...
129	CARROWMORE HALT N	7	10	14	15	6 17	6 22	...	...	...	...	...	...	7 56	7 57	...	...	...	...
134½	LEYNY ... + ¶	7	11	13	14	6 39	6 49	...	...	...	...	...	...	8 06	8 07	...	...	...	...
139	COLLOONEY HALT W	6	7	12	12	7 05	7 17	...	...	...	...	...	...	8 15	8 16	...	...	...	...
140¾	BALLYSODARE ¶	3	3	6	6	7 27	7 45	...	...	...	...	...	...	8 21	8 23	...	...	...	...
145¼	**SLIGO** ... ¶ W ●	**8**	**8**	**16**	**15**	**8 05**	...	...	...	...	...	...	...	**8 35**	...	...	...	...	...

C.R.—Stops to pick up or set down when required.

M.*—Scheduled Mail Train between Limerick and Ennis only. M.—Scheduled Mail Train.

12 June 1961 to 10 September 1961

27

SLIGO TO TUAM, ENNIS AND LIMERICK

Distance from Sligo	DOWN TRAINS		8 Sectional Running Pas. D	8 Pas. S	8 Gds. D	8 Gds. S	9 PAS. Loco. D.E. arr.	9 dep.	10 Galway PAS. D.E. arr.	10 dep.	11 Goods Loco. D.E. arr.	11 dep.	12 Goods Loco. D.E. arr.	12 dep.	13 D.E. PAS. M* arr.	13 dep.	14 PAS. M Loco. D.E. arr.	14 dep.	15 PAS. D.E. arr.	15 dep.
							WEEK-DAYS													
Mls.							a.m.	a.m.	a.m.	a.m.	a.m.	a.m.	a.m.	a.m.	a.m.	a.m.	p.m.	p.m.	p.m.	p.m.
—	**SLIGO** ...	W ●	**0**	**0**	**0**	**0**	...	...	...	...	...	...	...	**6 45**	...	**8 50**	...	...	...	...
4½	BALLYSODARE	...	8	8	10	15	...	...	...	...	...	...	6 59	7 20	9 00	9 01	...	...	...	...
6¼	COLLOONEY ...	W	3	3	6	6	...	...	...	...	...	...	7 30	7 45	9 06	9 07	...	...	...	...
10¾	LEYNY ...	+	9	10	14	18	...	...	...	...	...	...	8 03	8 10	9 18	9 19	...	...	...	...
16½	CARROWMORE	N	9	11	17	20	...	...	...	...	...	...	8 31	8 36	9 30	9 31	...	...	...	...
21¼	TUBBERCURRY	W	7	10	15	16	...	...	...	...	...	...	8 55	9 57	9 40	9 41	...	...	...	...
25	CURRY ...	N	5	7	10	10	...	...	...	...	...	...	10 11	10 16	9 48	9 49	...	...	...	...
27¾	CHARLESTOWN	+	4	6	8	9	...	...	...	...	...	...	10 28	10 48	9 55	9 56	...	...	...	...
34¾	SWINFORD ...	W	8	14	17	21	...	...	...	...	...	...	11 09	11 39	10 06	10 07	...	...	...	...
42½	KILTIMAGH ...	...	10	15	18	20	...	...	...	...	...	...	12 01	12 30	10 19	10 20	...	...	...	...
52	**CLAREMORRIS**	U W ●	**13**	**18**	**21**	**27**	...	...	...	...	...	**7 00**	**12 55**	**1 45**	**10 35**	**10 52**	...	...	...	...
56½	BALLINDINE ...	+	6	7	11	11	...	...	...	...	...	7 13	2 00	2 20	11 00	11 01	...	...	...	...
60¼	MILLTOWN (GALWAY)	...	5	6	9	9	...	...	...	...	...	7 22	2 33	2 53	11 08	11 09	...	...	...	...
64½	CASTLEGROVE	...	5	7	10	10	...	...	...	...	...	7 32	3 07	3 12	11 16	11 17	...	...	...	...
									From											
69¼	**TUAM** ...	U W ●	**6**	**7**	**10**	**12**	...	**7 55**	Galway		**7 44**	**8 10**	**3 26**	**4 10**	**11 25**	**11 29**	...	**3 35**	...	**9 20**
75½	BALLYGLUNIN	...	8	11	17	20	8 05	8 06	...	...	...	8 29	4 31	4 37	11 39	11 40	3 45	3 47	C.R.	
84¾	**ATHENRY**	W ●	**11**	**16**	**24**	**29**	**8 19**	**8 23**	**9 22**	**9 31**	**8 55**	**10 15**	**5 05**	**6 30**	**11 53**	**12 21**	**4 00**	**4 08**	**9 43**	...
90¼	CRAUGHWELL	+	7	9	13	13	...	...	9 40	9 41	10 32	10 42	...	6 45	12 30	12 32	...	...	...	...
96¼	ARDRAHAN ...	+	8	9	15	18	...	...	9 51	9 52	11 01	11 16	...	7 00	12 42	12 44	...	...	...	...
103	GORT	W	9	10	15	17	...	...	10 03	10 05	11 35	12 05	7 17	7 27	12 55	12 59	...	...	...	...
108½	TUBBER ...	...	7	7	12	13	...	...	10 14	10 15	C.R.	12 20	...	7 42	1 08	1 09	...	...	...	...
112¾	CRUSHEEN ...	...	6	7	11	12	...	...	10 23	10 24	12 35	12 43	...	7 53	1 17	1 18	...	...	...	...
120½	**ENNIS** ...	W ●	**10**	**12**	**18**	**19**	...	...	**10 36**	**10 45**	**1 05**	**5 00**	**8 13**	**8 50**	**1 30**	**1 40**	...	...	...	...
122½	CLARECASTLE	...	3	3	6	6	...	...	10 50	10 51	5 10	5 20	...	8 58	1 45	1 46	...	...	...	...
125½	ARDSOLLUS	...	4	5	11	12	...	...	10 57	10 58	...	5 33	...	9 09	1 52	1 53	...	...	...	...
128¾	BALLYCAR ...	+	5	6	9	10	...	...	11 05	11 06	5 44	5 54	...	9 18	2 00	2 01	...	...	...	...
132¼	SIXMILEBRIDGE	...	4	5	10	10	...	...	11 12	11 13	6 08	6 23	...	9 28	2 07	2 08	...	...	...	...
135½	CRATLOE HALT	...	4	4	9	12	...	...	11 19	11 20	...	6 34	...	9 37	2 14	2 15	...	...	...	...
141¼	LONGPAVEMENT HALT	+	7	8	15	15	...	...	C.R.		...	6 49	...	9 52	2 24	2 25	...	...	...	...
144¾	LIMERICK (CHECK)	...	...	...	...	...	...	...	...	...	...	6 59	...	...	...	...	...	...	...	...
145½	**LIMERICK**	●	**7**	**7**	**11**	**12**	...	...	**11 40**	...	**7 05**	...	**10 05**	...	**2 35**	...	...	...	...	...

C.R.—Stops to pick up or set down when required. N—No Telephone Communication. M.*—Scheduled Mail Train between Ennis and Limerick only. M—Scheduled Mail Train.

TRACK PLANS

The following track plans, which are not to scale, show several stations along the route as they were in the 1960s – though they would have altered little if at all throughout the life of the railway until very recent times. The track plan at Tubbercurry is typical of a medium-sized station on the route, while Claremorris and Athenry are included as they were major junctions.

Small stations on the line often had but a single platform, a small station building which doubled as the stationmaster's private residence, and perhaps one or two sidings for goods traffic, along with a small store.

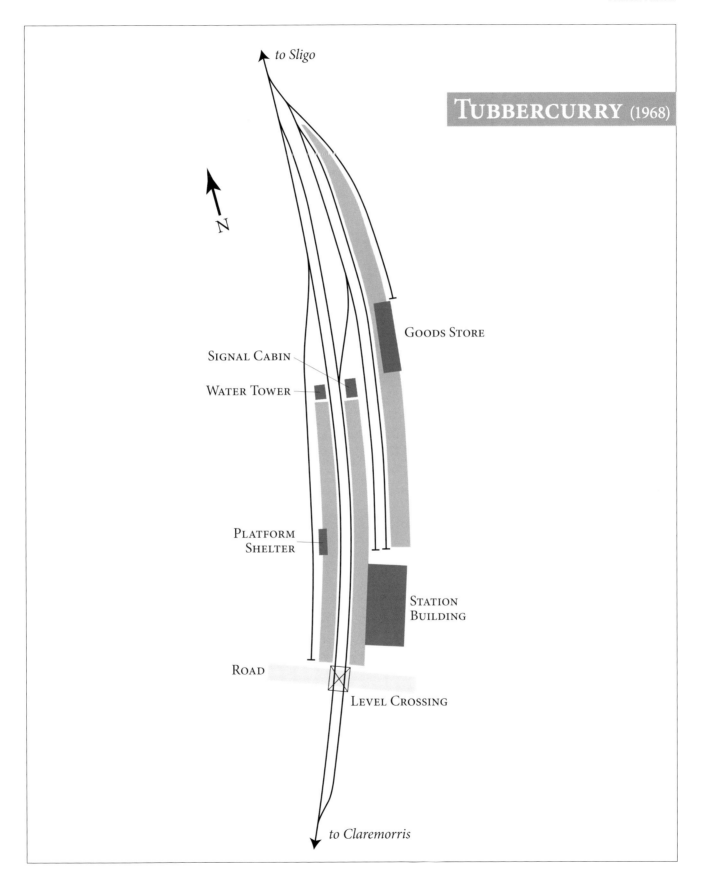

to Sligo

N

TUBBERCURRY (1968)

GOODS STORE

SIGNAL CABIN

WATER TOWER

PLATFORM
SHELTER

STATION
BUILDING

ROAD

LEVEL CROSSING

to Claremorris

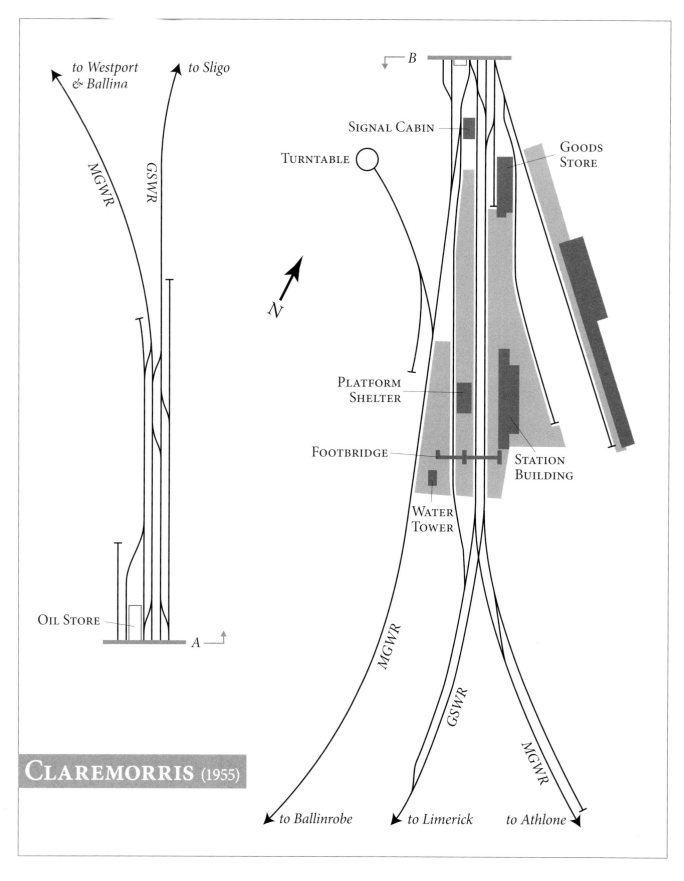

to Westport
& Ballina

to Sligo

MGWR

GSWR

B

SIGNAL CABIN

GOODS
STORE

TURNTABLE

N

PLATFORM
SHELTER

FOOTBRIDGE

STATION
BUILDING

WATER
TOWER

OIL STORE

A

MGWR

GSWR

MGWR

CLAREMORRIS (1955)

to Ballinrobe

to Limerick

to Athlone

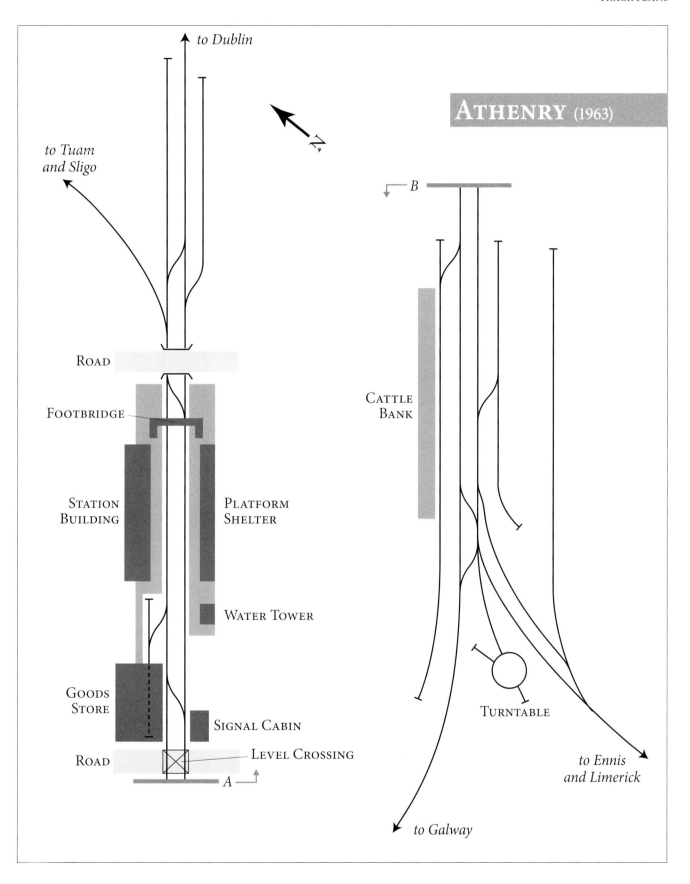

to Dublin

to Tuam
and Sligo

N

ROAD

FOOTBRIDGE

STATION
BUILDING

PLATFORM
SHELTER

WATER TOWER

GOODS
STORE

SIGNAL CABIN

ROAD

LEVEL CROSSING

A

ATHENRY (1963)

B

CATTLE
BANK

TURNTABLE

to Ennis
and Limerick

to Galway

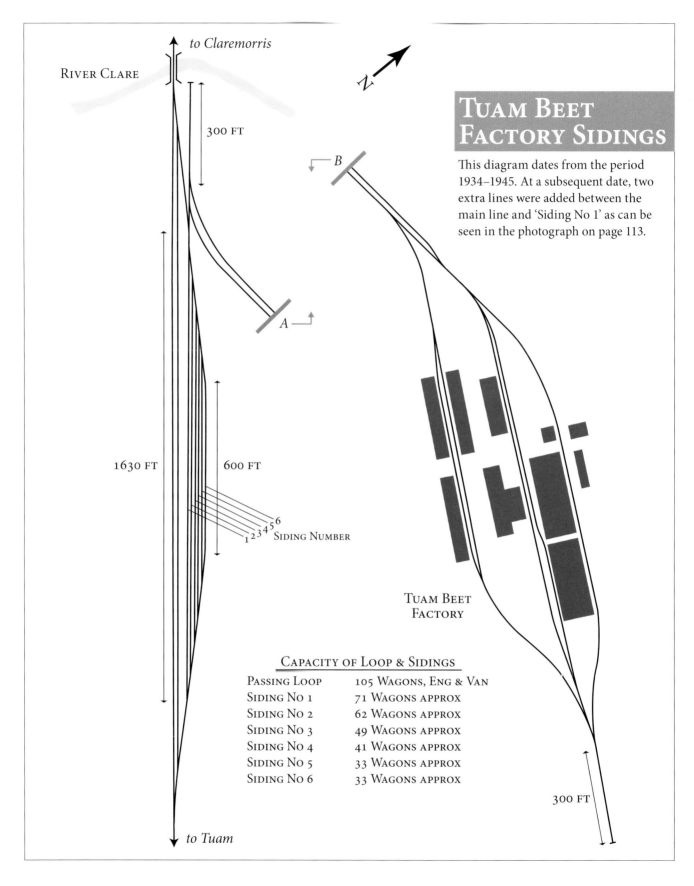

to Claremorris

RIVER CLARE

300 FT

N

TUAM BEET FACTORY SIDINGS

This diagram dates from the period 1934–1945. At a subsequent date, two extra lines were added between the main line and 'Siding No 1' as can be seen in the photograph on page 113.

B

A

1630 FT

600 FT

6
5
4
3
2
1 SIDING NUMBER

TUAM BEET FACTORY

CAPACITY OF LOOP & SIDINGS

PASSING LOOP	105 WAGONS, ENG & VAN
SIDING NO 1	71 WAGONS APPROX
SIDING NO 2	62 WAGONS APPROX
SIDING NO 3	49 WAGONS APPROX
SIDING NO 4	41 WAGONS APPROX
SIDING NO 5	33 WAGONS APPROX
SIDING NO 6	33 WAGONS APPROX

300 FT

to Tuam

Locomotives Used on this Route

Rather than give repetitive details of each locomotive shown in each picture caption, what follows is a broad description of those referred to. Detailed accounts of each class and its technical characteristics belong elsewhere, therefore this is not an exhaustive treatise on all CIÉ locomotives.

Initially, CIÉ diesel locomotives had their numbers prefixed by a letter denoting the power classification, starting with 'A' for the most powerful. Within the 'B' range were locos of several types – most notably the four varieties delivered from General Motors, La Grange, Illinois, during the 1960s, and up to 1976.

After 1972 the letter prefixes were dropped as shown below. The relevant classes are:

'A' or 001-class: A1–A60, later 001–060

CIÉ's first mass-produced class of main line diesel locomotives, the first of the class of sixty were introduced between 1955 and 1957, and the last working examples were withdrawn in 1995. Several survive in preservation, one (A39) in working order on the Downpatrick and Co Down (heritage) Railway in Co Down. A55 is the star attraction in Hell's Kitchen bar and Railway Museum in Castlerea, Co Roscommon. The Irish Traction Group own A39, and they and the West Clare Railway have assured homes for A15 and A3 as well. These engines were commonplace on the Limerick to Sligo line on heavier trains, and were widely used on all duties elsewhere in Ireland. Built by Metropolitan Vickers, they initially had Crossley engines which proved very unreliable and troublesome, but new General Motors engines were installed in the late 1960s and early 1970s, transforming their reliability and usefulness, and enabling them to enjoy many more years of service.

'C' class: C201–C234, later 201–234

These were smaller versions of the 'A' class, delivered between 1956 and 1958 for use on lighter duties and branch lines. As branch lines closed, they graduated towards maintenance trains and after being re-engined along with the 'A' class, most were used on Dublin area suburban trains until the advent of the electrified 'DART' system in 1984. The last working example of the class retired in 1986. Two are preserved, in the care of the Irish Traction Group, and it is hoped that at least one will return to full working order.

Under the general classification of 'B', there were several variants.

B101 class: B101–B112, later 101–112

Built by the Birmingham Railway Carriage and Wagon Co, with Sulzer engines, these engines spent most of their working lives on the southern lines of CIÉ, though occasional forays up the Limerick–Sligo route were made. Introduced between 1956 and 1957, the last (106) was withdrawn in 1978. In later years the 'Birmingham Sulzers' were little used, though consideration had been given to re-engining them with GM units at one time.

121-class: B121–132, later 121–132

The first American built diesel locomotives in Ireland (in 1961), which set a trend for CIÉ in that all subsequent locomotive orders have been from General Motors, and, since the three 'Hunslet' locomotives of 1970, Northern Ireland Railways has also stuck with GM products to this day. The 121-class had a single cab and were a development of a standard American 'switcher' design of locomotive. The last two examples of the 121-class were in use until 2008 and have been saved for possible preservation.

141-class: B141–B177, later 141–177

Entering traffic between 1962 and 1963, these locos were broadly similar to the 121-class, except for having a cab at either end. This became the norm for all subsequent deliveries of locomotives. The last 141 in traffic was withdrawn in 2011. One 141 is preserved at Moyasta in Co Clare by the West Clare Railway, while the Railway Preservation Society of Ireland owns two 141s, and the Irish Traction Group has one. These last three are largely in working order.

181-class: B181–B192, later 181–192

These were a more powerful version of the 141-class, introduced in 1966. The last member of the class was withdrawn in 2009. One sample is preserved by the West Clare Railway, at Moyasta in Co Clare.

'G' class: G601–3, and G611–7

These were small four-wheeled Deutz-built shunting locomotives, three being delivered between 1956 and 1957, and another seven in 1962. In the context of this book, they were used on shunting duties at Limerick, and at the Sugar Factory in Tuam when their own diesel shunting locomotives were not available. The last 'G' class locomotives were withdrawn in 1977, though by that stage little use was being made of them. No fewer than five are preserved. The Irish Traction Group has four, two of which are in store, and two that are in use on the Downpatrick & Co Down Railway. The DCDR also own one. The three at Downpatrick form a pool of which one or two are generally in working order for shunting and works trains there.

071-class: 071–088

These engines were delivered after the letter prefixes had been discontinued in 1976, and all entered traffic in 1977 and remain in use. Larger and more powerful version of

the 141/181-class family, they were not regular visitors to the Limerick–Sligo line, and indeed the section north of Claremorris was already closed by the time they entered traffic. However, they have made occasional visits to the line, usually on enthusiast special trains.

201-class: 201–234

Built 1994/5 by GM, this time in Canada rather than Illinois, these locomotives carry out main line passenger and goods duties across the modern Iarnród Éireann network. Though very rarely, they have been seen between Limerick and Ennis in recent years before the Mk 3 carriages were withdrawn.

J15 class 0-6-0 steam locomotive

While Limerick to Sligo services were in the hands of the Waterford, Limerick & Western Railway prior to the GSWR takeover, locomotives from the latter company became commonplace on the line subsequently. As far back as 1917, Tuam shed was home to an allocation of six J15 class 0-6-0 steam locomotives, according to the late Billy Lohan, who had been based there as a fireman. In steam days the line had, as one might expect, been operated by a mixture of these and various steam locos of former Waterford, Limerick & Western Railway origin.

Passenger carriages and goods wagons

Passenger carriages and goods wagons featured in the pictures in this book are a general mix of the standard CIÉ 'Laminate', 'Park Royal' and 'Craven' designs of the day. Most of these carriage types dated from the mid-1950s. Carriages designed in the 1930s by the Great Southern Railway's Edgar C Bredin also feature in some trains shown, particularly pre-1980.

'WESTERN RAIL CORRIDOR' RE-OPENING

Prior to the latest incarnation of the Athenry to Ennis line as a Limerick–Galway Intercity route, and the campaign to reopen the whole line in recent years, the term 'Western Rail Corridor' had not been heard of! However, it is an appropriate description of the line.

Work started on re-laying the track between Ennis and Athenry during the summer of 2007. This was Phase 1 of the project to re-open eventually right through from Limerick to Sligo. Phase 2 would cover Athenry to Tuam whilst Phase 3 refers to Tuam to Claremorris. Originally, completion date was expected to be 2011 for Phase 2 and 2014 for Phase 3 but at the time of writing (in 2011) no work has commenced yet.

Phase 1 cost €106 million and this investment covered track, bridges, signals, level crossings and stations at Sixmilebridge, Gort, Ardrahan and Craughwell.

Excavations were made under overbridges to lower the trackbed for new track. Old track panels were removed and new drains installed. Excavations were made at cuttings to improve views at level crossings and the excavated materials were used for side filling at embankments.

In October 2007 beam re-laying started at Craughwell and three miles of CWR (Continuous Welded Rail) were quickly laid on concrete sleepers towards Athenry. The relaying train, the LWR (Long Welded Rail) train were common sights travelling from Portlaoise via Portarlington and Athenry. As time went on there were also deliveries by road of Turkington concrete sleepers to Gort and they were loaded on to the re-laying train for use southwards. Ballast trains used many locations to load, for example north of Craughwell (see photograph on page 39), just south of Ardrahan station, Tubber and Crusheen.

Tubber bog proved to be a difficult area from an engineering point of view. This was dealt with by clearing and repairing the existing drainage, placing a tensar sheet on the trackbed, and piling in a zoom section on poor ground. With pile driving completed between Tubber station and Gortavogher level crossing the final section of track had been laid in the overall project by early summer 2009. Therefore welding could continue on the large number of joints to be attended to.

Between Ennis and Athenry there were 126 level crossings on the 36 mile section. As far as possible many of these were closed and after the usual planning permission procedures they were replaced by new overbridges and access roads.

It is proposed to reopen a station at Oranmore, on the Athenry to Galway line. This is indicated on the maps in the railcars travelling from Limerick to Galway. When complete, the new station will be located at Garraun level crossing which is about ¾ mile west of the former station and block post at Oranmore, closed in 1963.

Another station to be reopened along the route is Crusheen, where local pressure to achieve this paid off. It had also been closed in 1963.

On 29 March 2010 a special train with politicians, railway officials and the Minister of Transport left Limerick at 1030 and called at all stations en route to Galway where short ceremonies occurred to mark the re-opening. Very large crowds welcomed the new service but they did this from the car parks as only authorised personnel were allowed on the platform while the train was there. The general public were not completely ignored, however, as for example in Gort a large tent was provided serving refreshments. Next day the full service was introduced with five trains each way Monday–Saturday, with four on Sundays. Journey time is typically about 1 hour 56 minutes but the first train from Limerick at 0600 initially had a 25 minute stop at Ennis for crossing purposes!

Traffic exceeded expectations and it was found that the two piece 2700-class railcars were inadequate on certain services and these were increased to three piece or four piece. The 1725 from Galway can be a very popular train. After the first month IE reported that 16,000 passengers were recorded and this was in addition to the 14,400 monthly journeys on the Limerick to Ennis Service.

Sixmilebridge, Gort, Ardrahan and Craughwell stations are now unmanned and are provided with ticket vending machines, CCTV and car parking. The platforms are 90m long. Gort has two platforms of 90m each together with a wheelchair accessible footbridge. Gort also has a lengthy loop and many of the services are scheduled to cross here. Others cross at Ennis.

It is to be hoped that continued patronage of the new service will lead to further expansion of passenger trains along the Western Rail Corridor in the future.

Opposite upper: On 18 February 2010 single unit 2753 is in use for driver training between Ennis and Galway, just north of the level crossing at Craughwell. Most Galway–Limerick services are now in the hands of 2700-class railcars.

The following six pictures were taken on 22 April 2010.

Opposite lower: Sixmilebridge, Co Clare, showing the newly reopened station. The 0945 Galway to Limerick pauses at the current platform, just north of the original station, which can be seen in the foreground. Many of the original station buildings along the line are now either derelict or in use as private residences. It is interesting to compare this picture with that on page 14, taken some 23 years earlier.

Opposite upper: Units 2705/6 coast through Tubber on the 1155 Limerick to Galway service. The nicely restored former station building is now a private house. One of the original platform signs can be seen, now displayed on the wall under the erstwhile platform canopy. On the left is one of the locations where ballast was loaded for the recently relaid track.

Opposite lower: 2714 leads the 1210 Galway to Limerick train. The new motorway is under construction in the background. Will railway timings compete in the future with frequent express buses?

Above: A two car 2700-class railcar leaves Ardrahan en route to Limerick. The train is the 1430 ex-Galway. This picture illustrates perfectly the old order and the new. To the left of the train green fields surrounded by traditional stone walls show typical lineside scenery since the line opened. To its right, the view is spoiled by excessive and obtrusive fencing, piles of stone and general suburban-style traffic facilities, despite the rural location.

Opposite upper: An updated version of the cover photograph. 2720/19 on the 1415 Limerick to Galway train passing Labane Castle. The stone wall visible on the cover photograph is still there, though overgrown and supplemented by a post and wire fence. Labane Castle is just south of Ardrahan.

Opposite lower: 2703 en route to Limerick about 3km south of Craughwell on the 0945 from Galway, 23 April 2010. To the right and left of the railcar can be seen the broken remains of the wooden sleepers cleared away during relaying of the track. The photographer visited the site the following morning and the wooden pieces were all cleared away.

Above: Gort, looking north, 23 April 2010. Single unit 2753 heads a three car train for Limerick. Many changes have taken place at this location since the line was previously in use. Most obvious is the position of the water tower, which had been moved back from the line to allow room for the passenger footpath seen in the foreground. The old platform was where the photographer is standing to take this picture, and the new platforms can be seen either side of the train. Obviously, the footbridge is also new. Train crews are often changed here now.

Opposite upper: The train shown on page 135 heads away from Gort. Many of the changes referred to in its caption will be evident by comparison of this photograph with that on page 30, which was taken in 1980. The former up platform (to the left of the track) has now been cleared away, though its remains can be seen as a bank of rubble. On the right, the goods shed is now closed up, and beyond that, just visible, is the former station building, no longer in railway use.

Opposite lower: 2713 heads a four car set on the 0935 ex-Limerick at milepost 50¾, just north of Ardrahan, on 24 April 2010. On busier services, trains are often strengthened to four cars, instead of the usual two or three. At this location, an overbridge (from which the picture was taken) has replaced the original (level) accommodation crossing to enable local landowners to cross the line safely.

Above: Probably the only working of a regular public train by an 071-class locomotive and Mk 3 coaching stock on the Western Rail Corridor. On 24 April 2010, the Irish Railway Record Society operated a special train from Dublin to Limerick, thence to Athenry and back to Dublin. Between Limerick and Ennis, this train took up the timetable path of the 1240 local train. As a result, the train was made available to routine public passengers between these points and at the intermediate station of Sixmilebridge. This picture is taken at Clarecastle. Another unique working past this location occurred on 28 February 1993; see picture on page 18. Remains of the former track lie at the base of the bridge abutment to the left of the picture.

Opposite upper: 2718, 2717 and single unit 2751 form the 1430 ex Galway on 29 July 2010. All three are in the new livery applied to these vehicles from around this time. The picture was taken at milepost 50¾. It will be noticed that the end gangway connection has now been closed up on the leading car, as it has been on some others. This train had been strengthened to three cars on account of the fact that this was Galway Races week. Others on this day had four cars.

Opposite lower: The 1210 Galway to Limerick train passes north of Craughwell, Co Galway, on 26 May 2011. The train is the now-typical two car 2700 series set. 2726 leads 2723. These railcars were built by GEC Alsthom, Spain. The order was placed in 1996 with delivery starting in early 1998. At the time of writing (2011) all of this class are based in Limerick for use on the Nenagh branch, the Waterford Line, and the shuttle service to Limerick Junction – as well as the Galway line. The gangway ends on these railcars have been blocked off in recent times.

Above: The annual 'spray train' near Craughwell on a rainy day, 26 May 2011, en route to Limerick. The converted coach in the centre of the train was previously a 'BR' generator van. The bridge is a new one, built to replace a former farmer's accommodation crossing. Many crossings have been treated in this way in recent times in order to eliminate the possibility of level crossing accidents, and livestock straying onto the track.

Opposite upper: The same train passes Crusheen. The former station is behind the photographer, but the level area in the foreground was used to load ballast during renewals of track in recent times.

Opposite lower: On the same day, the 'spray train' awaits the road in Ennis, as the 1415 Limerick to Galway railcar approaches. On this date the 1500 Ennis to Limerick train was replaced by buses in order to provide a timetable path for the weedspraying train.

Above: 2717 leads 2718, forming the 1415 Limerick to Galway train in Ennis, 26 May 2011. The former West Clare narrow gauge trains left from the right hand side of the platform, along which a fence has now been erected. The goods yard used to be on the right.

Above: A Limerick bound train in Ennis, 20 August 2011. The recently blocked-off gangway end on railcar 2724 looks somewhat unattractive, as it has not yet been painted. On the left hand (down) platform, the steam-era water crane may still be seen, now looking quite out of place in such a modern setting.

And finally...

While the last two pictures are not in colour, they show Ennis station as it was while the narrow gauge West Clare line was still operating, just prior to the period covered in the book.

Opposite upper: The Sligo to Limerick train arrives in Ennis, summer 1962. There is much of interest to be seen here. On the left two double deck buses, one in the then-new navy blue and cream livery, the other still in two tone green. In the background, former West Clare Railway No 5 is plinthed as a static exhibit. The whole area to the left of the train was the terminus of the erstwhile West Clare narrow gauge line to Kilrush and Kilkee, closed in January 1961. The then-new 121-class loco hauling the train is in its original light grey and yellow livery (as shown on the rear cover). Behind it, a four-wheel guard's van is followed by a standard 'laminate' coach of the day – then quite new – and behind that a more venerable 1930s era 'Bredin' design coach of Great Southern Railways ancestry. Taking up the rear is another four-wheel guard's van, still in its original unpainted aluminium 'livery', followed by two cattle trucks. *(John Langford)*

Opposite lower: A busy scene at Ennis before the West Clare narrow gauge line was closed. The cattle train in the foreground is bound for Limerick, and behind it the locomotive of the northbound train to Sligo is blowing off steam. On the right, three West Clare carriages sit at the platform awaiting their locomotive to take them to Kilrush or Kilkee, as immortalised in Percy French's song, "Are ye right there Michael, are ye right". The West Clare line, by now the West Clare Section (as it was known) of CIÉ, was fully dieselised in 1955, the only Irish narrow gauge line ever to be fully modernised. However, it fell victim to the accountant's pen in January 1961, surviving to become the last public narrow gauge line in the country. On the extreme left a CIÉ lorry awaits its next duty in the goods yard. *(John Langford)*

If you enjoyed reading this book, then these Colourpoint publications may also be of interest.

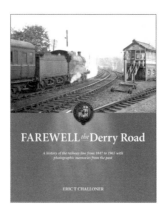

**FAREWELL THE
DERRY ROAD**

Eric Challoner – 978 1 906578 76 3

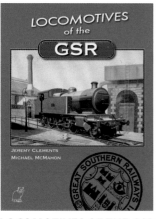

LOCOMOTIVES OF THE GSR

*Clements & McMahon –
978 1 906578 26 8*

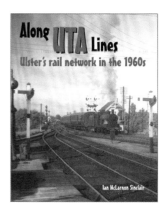

**ALONG UTA LINES – Ulster's
Rail Network in the 1960s**

Ian Sinclair – 978 1 906578 49 7

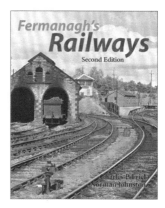

FERMANAGH'S RAILWAYS

*Friel & Johnston –
978 1 906578 16 9*

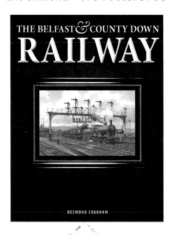

**THE BELFAST & COUNTY
DOWN RAILWAY**

Des Coakham – 978 1 906578 73 2

'THE WEE DONEGAL' REVISITED

*Robotham & Curran –
978 1 904242 02 4*

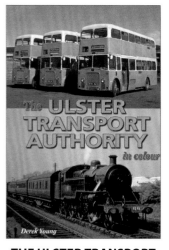

**THE ULSTER TRANSPORT
AUTHORITY IN COLOUR**

Derek Young – 978 1 904242 66 6

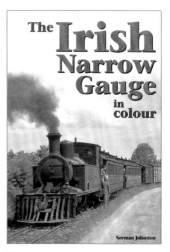

**THE IRISH NARROW GAUGE
IN COLOUR**

N Johnston – 978 1 904242 13 0

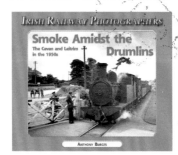

**SMOKE AMIDST THE
DRUMLINS – The Cavan &
Leitrim in the 1950s**

Anthony Burges
978 1 904242 62 8

**STEAM IN ULSTER IN
THE 1960s**

Ian Sinclair & Richard Whitford
978 1 904242 83 3

**THE SWILLY AND THE WEE
DONEGAL**

Anthony Burges
978 1 904242 63 5

**CHASING THE FLYING SNAIL
CIÉ operations in the 1950s**

Anthony Burges
978 1 904242 51 2